"I felt like the luckiest person on earth when I not only met Chawade[...] food navigator through Bangkok. We walked, boated, and ate our wa[...] I've ever had, all thanks to Chawadee, her warmth and expertise. An[...] best thing: her fantastic book. Enjoy every delicious bite."—Phil Ros[...]

"After traveling to Thailand for many years to eat, I found Chawadee's *Bangkok's Fifty Best Food Stalls* book online and had the temerity to contact her, hoping for suggestions. Next thing I knew I made a friend for life. But more importantly, I had the best guide to eating in Thailand a Thai food fanatic could ask for. Her palate should be declared a National Treasure.—**Robert Mark Kamen**, screenwriter and creator of *The Karate Kid, Fifth Element, The Transporter* and *Taken*

"*Real Thai Cooking* covers many of the popular dishes that people in Thailand eat on a day to day basis, dissected into recipes, with stories and detailed explanations to help them make sense. From ingredients, to meal plans, recipes, and valuable Thai cultural context, *Real Thai Cooking* is a fantastic overview into the world of Thai food, and how you can make it at home."—**Mark Wiens**, migrationology.com

"The variety of Thai street food is so wide that this cookbook will be your best friend to help explore safely the secret flavours of Thai cuisine and not to miss any."—**Stephane Junca**, director of Secret Retreats (secret-retreats.com)

"This book made me want to jump on a plane and eat my way round Thailand again—and this time, I would finally come to understand the secrets of Thai food customs. . . *Real Thai Cooking* is a must-have for any serious Thai food lover!"—**Anne Faber**, presenter of "Anne's Kitchen" and author of *My Luxembourg: Home Sweet Home*

"*Real Thai Cooking* is a fitting name for this well crafted, accurately detailed, regional, cultural and sometimes historical account of the food I love. Chow's knowledge and passion for Thai cuisine flows from these pages with insights and reflections that offer a nuanced understanding of the many aspects of the Thai culinary landscape."—**Dylan Jones**, chef and co-owner of Err and The Food Trust

"What an easy book to like. And what a wonderful book to read and learn to love Thai food. I'm seduced ... "—**David Thompson**, chef and author of *Thai Food*

"Chawadee's new book *Real Thai Cooking* brings back childhood memories of fabulous foods that are classic and authentic. She has traipsed each region of Thailand and taken their culinary highlights and different cooking styles from family to street, from homegrown to hybrid. It's filled with interesting anecdotes on ingredients, history, recipes and, not to mention, mouth-watering photos of colourful and flavourful food."—**Thomas Vitayakul**, academic and owner of Ruen Urai

REAL THAI COOKING

RECIPES AND STORIES FROM A THAI FOOD EXPERT

Chawadee Nualkhair

Lauren Lulu Taylor

Foreword by Chef McDang

TUTTLE Publishing

Tokyo | Rutland, Vermont | Singapore

Contents

Food as a Window onto Thai Life and Culture

By Chef McDang

Chow and I go back a long long way. When I first met her, I was writing my own English-language Thai cooking bible, the *Principles of Thai Cookery*. I had written many cookbooks before then, but they were always in the Thai language, and I was wary that a cookbook in the English language would be sapped of all of my personality and sense of humor. Luckily, Chow was able to help me retain my voice in the text, and I could tell that she, too, felt as passionate about Thai cooking as I did. During the many, many hours we spent together while writing—she typing, me relating my recipes and the stories behind them—she was like a sponge, the perfect conduit for absorbing all of the information from my brain onto the page. I am happy to have had such a good pupil of Thai culinary history.

Since then, we have managed to keep in touch. Over the years, as she has written various articles on Thai cuisine, she has asked me very specific and in-depth questions about the history behind the food. I can see that her interest in the cuisine and culture, like mine, is not superficial, and that she truly wants to know the context behind the food that the Thai people eat. In this way, she and I share a similar view of the cuisine, not just simply a way for people to get together and enjoy their lives, but as a mirror for the historical and social developments of a certain place and time. Thai food is delicious, but each dish is also a piece of history. I think it is important for people who take an interest in Thai food to approach the cuisine through this historical lens, and I know Chow shares the same sentiments.

I am so glad to see that Chow is finally coming out with her own book, which I am sure will be interesting and, at the same time, informative. I have always told Chow that I am a teacher and getting old and there are many ways to impart knowledge of Thai cuisine. I feel that my way of writing is a little stuffy and technical, and I am sure Chow's book will be a lot more fun and interesting as well as informative. I wish Chow all the success with this book and look forward to reading the whole book.

Exploring Thailand's Many Regional Cooking Styles

It's hard to understand from many Thai restaurant menus abroad, but needless to say, not everyone eats green curry and *pad Thai* on a regular basis. When it comes to food, Thailand is more of a patchwork quilt of regional styles, each part mirroring its own specific influences: China and Burma in the North; Laos in the Northeast; Malaysia and China in the South; and in the central region, all of the foreign influences disseminated by the Palace.

So we will explore Thailand like many have never seen it, region by region. Along the winding mountain roads up North, where travelers by car risk motion sickness when driving from one town to the next, open-air eateries abound with minced salads of meats and spices, eaten by hand with fresh leaves gathered in the mountains and bamboo baskets of sticky rice. The rice is meant to be rolled up into a ball, the edible receptacle by which to bring bits of *larb* or deep-fried pork to the mouth, in a motion known in Thai as *pun khao* (rolling rice).

Due to the North's "cooler" climate (of course, everything is relative), meals are of a heartier and, shall we say, meatier disposition. Platters are laden with fried herbaceous sausages known as *sai oua*, flattened schnitzel-like strips of pork called *moo pan*, and various other iterations of *moo tod* (deep-fried pork cutlets), which litter tables groaning under mountains of freshly steamed sticky rice. Here, the chicken may be cheap and the buffalo too hard at work to be eaten, but the pig reigns supreme.

Maybe because of its meat-for-ward diet, the North also tends to harbor much milder dishes, making it one of the less spicy of Thailand's regions. Even its chili dips—most famously, the *nam prik num* (roasted green chili dip) and *nam prik ong*, a Bolognese-like dip flavored with fermented bean paste—fall on the beginners' end of the spice spectrum, flavorings to augment the pork, bitter forest greens, tart soups, deep-fried pork rinds and sticky rice that form the bulk of Northern Thai cuisine.

And bitterness forms the insistent background chatter to the symphony of flavors that make up the food in the North. Marshalled by a plethora of herbs and other greens that grow naturally in the mountains, stews, minced salads, stir-fries and chili dips use the bitterness to highlight other ingredients' sweetness, and sometimes help that bitterness along with a helpful drop or two of *nam dee* (pork or beef bile).

The terrain is different in the Northeast, also known as "Isaan." The land—dusty, dry and rocky— is where the people work hard to scrape a living from the soil. Yet their food is as popular as anything else in Thailand, thanks to its direct, gregarious, and uncompromising flavors: spicy, tart and salty. Isaan cuisine is notorious for its aversion to sugar (something Bangkokians could not possibly live without) and its base of fermented fish known as *pla rah*. In fact, the saying goes that if it doesn't have *pla rah* in it, it's not really Isaan.

The cooking methods in the Northeast are, for the most part, quick and easy. Isaan people love food, but they also have better things to do. Grilling and boiling are what form the better part of these dishes, but there are also quite a few shredded salads (the most famous of which is *som tum*), made up quickly in a mortar and pestle. Everything is accompanied by local herbs such as *pak chee farang* (sawtooth coriander) and *pak chee lao*

(dill) as well as fresh cut long beans and a spice-fighting wedge of juicy fresh cabbage.

And unlike in the North, the fire in this cuisine is real. Although the staple here is also sticky rice, Isaan food might rank as the second spiciest in the land, incorporating copious amounts of chilies into their dips, salads, stews and sauces. Maybe this is why the Isaan word *saap* (for "spicy" and "delicious") are the same.

When I say that Isaan food is the second-spiciest in Thailand, it's only because the South exists. Think of the spiciest food you have ever had, and then multiply that by 10. While Isaan food may make your nose run and your eyes water, Southern Thai food will set your ears ringing and make your head feel lighter on your shoulders. Southern Thai chefs like to say that their food is the food of the "soldiers" (i.e. cheap). What they mean by that is that the food is so spicy that copious amounts of plain steamed rice must be eaten, thereby filling up the stomach more quickly and cheaply.

The South is known for its seafood, but its history is far richer than that. The bulk of Thailand's Muslim community calls the South home, and are centered in Thailand's three southernmost provinces: Yala, Narathiwat, and Pattani, which were once known as part of the Sultanate of Pattani. It was taken over by Siam in 1785 and, since 2001, remains riven by conflict. All the same, the Malaysian influence thrums insistently throughout the region's cuisine, resulting in the liberal use of turmeric and dried spices.

The South is also host to some of the country's most vibrant Chinese enclaves. The site of a thriving tin mining industry, places like Phuket welcomed Hokkien Chinese communities to its increasingly wealthy shores, resulting in a number of dishes that cannot be found anywhere else in Thailand. Meanwhile, sizable Teochew communities sprouted in various parts along the Southern Thai coastline, resulting in fusion Chinese-Thai treatments of seafood—steamed fish in soy sauce, shellfish baked with glass vermicelli—that have become key components of the mainstream Thai menu today. Let's not forget the invention of a little-known sauce called Sriracha, named after a Southern Thai coastal town. Although Americans may be familiar with a Vietnamese-American version of the sauce, the inspiration for that sauce is Chinese-Thai: tart, spicy and sweet, brewed from chilies aged in the sun.

Surprisingly, it's in the central region where we may find the most revelations. Yes, we all know about pork satay and chicken with cashew nuts. We've had plenty of massaman curry and fried rice in a pineapple. But there are dishes that have been carved out of the region's unique history that few casual diners really know.

Known as the "rice basket" of the country, the verdant Central region is incredibly fertile, spawning papayas, bananas, pineapples, limes, and of course rice with ease. Indeed, this region is so fertile that it has formed part of the Thai national identity; one of the first inscriptions in the Thai language reads: "In the time of King Ramkhamhaeng the Great, this land of Sukhothai is thriving. There is fish in the water and rice in the fields." This inscription, one of the oldest discovered so far, fuels the belief that as long as rice continues to grow and fish continue to swim, Thais will never go hungry.

The northern reaches of the region, home to both Sukhothai and Ayutthaya, another of the kingdom's former capitals, boast abundant access to limes, palm sugar, tamarind and fish, dictating a flavor profile that today is considered distinctly Thai. Sweet, spicy, tart, salty, umami and a little bitter, the coexistence of these tastes on one spoon is called *rot grom* (rounded flavors) in Thai. These are the flavors that have traveled worldwide and made Thai cuisine famous.

Meanwhile, Thailand has shown a unique talent for incorporating whatever foreign influences reach it, tweaking them, and assimilating them into something completely different and ultimately Thai. In the age of the Sukhothai and Ayutthaya kings, foreign envoys from lands as far-flung as Portugal and Persia brought with them chilies, corn, and peanuts—ingredients that would one day be wholeheartedly associated with Thailand. Shrimp paste and fish sauce arrived courtesy of Arabic traders or Chinese merchants, depending on which food historian you talk to. A foreign cook by the name of Maria Guyomar de Pinha even came to work in the palace, bringing with her new cooking techniques like steaming flour "cupcakes" for desserts and new ways of using common ingredients like eggs. Instead of blocking off these influences, Thailand welcomed them with the knowledge that they would take on a Thai twist in time.

Since then, Thailand's most recent capital, Bangkok, continues to host culinary innovations of its own. An influx of Chinese immigrants in the mid-1800s to mid-1900s led government authorities to engineer their own ways to turn typical "Chinese" ingredients like noodles into something more closely resembling Thais' views of their own food. This directly led to dishes like *pad Thai*. Even when left to flourish on its own, Chinese influence on Thai cuisine—woks, frying, deep-frying, duck meat—eventually took on distinctly Thai identities, leading to fusion dishes as varied as *pad see ew* (noodles stir-fried in soy sauce) and *gang phed ped yang* (grilled duck red curry). Today, the traditionally "Chinese" dishes enjoyed by Thais like *khao thom* (rice porridge), *joke* (rice congee), soup noodles and dim sum have taken on flavors and garnishes that actual Chinese diners would find bizarre.

Of course, a discussion of Chinese influence on Thai food cannot be complete without touching on street food. Chinese workers who came to Thailand found themselves shut off from traditional avenues of employment like the civil service, forcing them into lower-paying jobs like construction. Because their homes were too small to allow them to cook in, they resorted to eat outside—resulting in rudimentary restaurants. Soon, food hawkers devoted their time to working the waterways that once criss-crossed the city, offering dishes once available in their hometowns, like soup noodles. Street food in Thailand was born.

While culinary innovations once emanated from the royal palace and the cooks who hosted its many foreign envoys, much of the inspiration for Thai food now arguably comes from the streets. Because of the low threshold involved in setting up a stall, it is the street that now sniffs out prominent trends like Japanese *takoyaki* or Korean *galbi*, fashioning them into

dishes palatable to Thai tastes. Recent attempts to curb street food—arrested by the current COVID outbreak—have threatened to upset a delicate ecosystem that not only benefited the Thai food scene, but the wallets of ordinary working Thais who make up a bulk of the city's workforce.

Today, Bangkok's Chinatown (also known as Yaowarat) is considered the spiritual heart of Thailand's street food scene, even if street food can (even now) be found on almost every corner. Chinatown is now a big business, hosting food tours and throngs of tourists, as well as nostalgic Bangkokians eager for a taste of their childhood. It is even the site of something of a food and drink renaissance, its picturesque qualities the perfect setting for new restaurants and bars seeking to refocus on Thai and Asian identities. Even with all of the upheaval that the world has undergone, innovation is burbling away in some Yaowarat alleyways.

Going forward, Thailand, like everywhere else, faces challenges it hasn't encountered before. The rapid pace of change wrought by the Internet, easy travel and global businesses have made cultural change seem out-of-control, leading to strange government decisions like the recent attempt to build a "Thai food tasting robot" to keep the standard taste of every Thai dish served in a restaurant the same.

Maybe not surprisingly, this met with less success than the cooking contest that led to *pad Thai*. All the same, globalization has also led to the drive to learn more by encouraging more home cooking and the placing of recipes in their proper historical and cultural contexts.

If this cookbook succeeds even a little bit in that, this jaded food writer will have considered herself blessed with plenty of rice in the field and fish in the water.

Food Secrets Only the Thais Know About

I was eight when I started cooking, and it was out of necessity. My father was normally the cook of the family, but as a pediatrician, he didn't get off work until eight at night, and that was sometimes too late for me. My mother's attempts at cooking were rare and better off forgotten, for both her and for us. If I was hungry and wanted to eat, I would have to do it myself.

We only had one cookbook, a well-worn tome from the 1970s full of recipes for aspics and salads suspended in jelly. But there were also important basics that formed the building blocks for what I grew to love about the act of cooking itself: the patient stirring of a sauce as it thickens, the layering of flavors and aromas in the pot, the selection and preparation of fresh ingredients perfectly suited to a dish.

When it came to writing my first cookbook, I wanted to translate that kind of love for food into my own pages. Because Thai food is so complex and varied, I imagined it would be a difficult task to undertake. But the truth is, the love of the food isn't hard to communicate. Thais, at their very heart, love their cuisine. For centuries, it has been the way for Thais to share between friends, to bond with would-have-been enemies, or to catch up with loved ones. "Kin khao la yang?" ("Have you eaten yet?" or, more accurately, "Have you eaten rice yet?") is still a common greeting. And even in the age of COVID, Thais still manage to share stories and jokes over a common meal, even if it's over the computer.

But make no mistake: COVID had a big impact on our lives here in Thailand, making it much harder for people to make those culinary connections face-to-face, to learn from each other over a shared countertop, or to laugh over kitchen disasters with a bottle of beer. All the more reason, then, for something like this cookbook—a part of Thailand that you can craft in your own kitchen. It might not be exactly like what you would find in Thailand, but that doesn't really matter. Honestly, I can't imagine something more Thai than taking a piece of Thailand and spinning it for yourself.

The fact is, the "secrets" promised above are things that everyone probably already knows. Let's face it: there are people who like to cook, but who are lazy. They are my brethren. But a desire to take things easy doesn't automatically mean the food will be bad. The "secrets," if you can call them that, are that good cooking comes from the heart. That what you attempt isn't always going to work. That there will be days when you just don't feel it, and that it's alright if that's the case. But if the love is always there, your explorations in the kitchen ultimately will not be in vain.

That said, there are rules that govern most Thai dishes. They remain rules that most Thais follow, even today. They are:

■ Thais only cook with unscented oils like vegetable, peanut and canola. That's because, like a chef averse to a strong cologne, no one wants to

fight through competing smells which will mess with their perceptions of taste, and the aromas for each dish are already strong.

- Thai food is served at room temperature, which probably seems odd to Westerners who prize hot food. This is because Thailand is a hot place.

- Thai food is served in bite-sized pieces, so there is no need for a knife at the place setting. Instead, diners eat with a fork and spoon. Food is served family style, with everyone partaking of the same large platter, with a central serving spoon for each dish.

- I've heard concern for "texture" thought of as an Asian thing. I find that a strange generalization. But if you are thinking that a "crunch" element is usually included in Thai cuisine, you would be right.

- Thais always cook on the bone, for more flavor. The decision to remove the bones before serving is up to the chef; I for one welcome it. There is nothing worse than biting down on a large juicy piece of fish in a nice *tom yum* and getting stabbed in the gums by a fish bone!

Menu Suggestions

These are some possible dinner menus that you can craft using the recipes in this book. You can either serve them in courses, as detailed below, or you can serve the appetizers and mains at the same time, family-style, with dessert after, like most of us do in Thailand. I'd suggest the best drink to go with these menus is beer (maybe even beer that's been left in the freezer until it's slushy, called *beer woon*), but Riesling and Gewurtztraminer are traditionally the wines said to go best with Thai food.

MENU 1
Thailand's Greatest Hits

APPETIZERS
Por Pia Tod Spring Rolls (page 109)
Tom Kha Gai Chicken Coconut Soup (page 65)
Fried Lacey Eggs with Thai-style Dressing (page 74)
Central Thai-style Fruit Som Tum (page 115)

MAINS
Pad Thai (page 52)
Khao Soy Curried Egg Noodles with Chicken (page 59)
Massaman Curry (page 136)
Steamed rice

DESSERT
Khao Niew Mamuang Mango Sticky Rice (page 144)

MENU 2
An Isaan Feast

APPETIZERS
Foolproof Som Tum Pla Rah (page 113)
Makuea Mashed Eggplant Salad (page 111)

MAINS
Gang Om Lemongrass and Dill Chicken Soup (page 110)
Mieng Pla Pow Baked Fish (page 118)
Grilled chicken with Jaew Chili Sauce (page 34)
Sticky Rice (page 90)

DESSERT
Fresh fruits like mango, pineapple, rose apple, and oranges

MENU 3
Street Food Favorites

APPETIZERS
Tom Yum Goong (page 67)
Or Suan Oyster Omelet (page 54)
Grilled Beef Meatballs with Sweet Chili Sauce (page 46)

MAINS
Pad Krapao Basil Stir Fry (page 45)
Drunken Noodles (page 50)

DESSERT
Coconut Ice Cream in Sweet Rolls (page 151)

MENU 4
Northern Thai Sampler

APPETIZERS
Saa Pak Northern Mixed Salad (page 87)
Nam Prik Ong Minced Pork dip (page 92)
Nam Prik Num Roasted Green Chili Dip (page 93)
Deep-fried Pork Rinds (page 131)

MAINS
Minced Pork or Beef Larb (page 98)
Pik Gai Tod Baab Fried Chicken Wings (page 91)
Nam Prik Tha Dang "Red Eye" Chili Dip (page 102)
Sai Oua Chiang Mai Sausage (page 95)
Sticky Rice (page 90)

DESSERT
Aunt Priew's Halo Halo (page 145)

MENU 5
A Retro Thai Meal

APPETIZERS
Nam Prik Kee Ga Dip (page 38)
Salmon Marinated in Nam Pla Fish Sauce
(page 64)
Gang Som Southern Fish Curry (page 127)

MAINS
Hearty Beef Tongue Stew (page 82)
Mee Krob Sweet and Sour Rice Noodles
(page 56)
Steamed rice (page 19)

DESSERT
Gluay Buad Chee Bananas in Sweet Coconut
Cream (page 143)

MENU 6
Southern Thai Seafood

APPETIZERS
Nam Prik Gapi Shrimp Paste Dip with Eggy
Eggplant and Moo Gon Pork Meatballs (page
36)
Yum Woon Sen Glass Vermicelli Salad (page 125)
Thai Oxtail Soup (page 135)

MAINS
Steamed seafood with Seafood Dipping Sauce
(page 33) or Seafood Sauce without Pickled
Garlic (page 33)
Shrimp in Curry-Egg Sauce (page 66)
Steamed rice (page 19)

DESSERT
Kanom Sai Gai Saffron-scented Jalebi (page 147)
Fresh fruits

MENU 7
When You're Hung Over

Khao Thom Rice Porridge (page 72)
Pickled Cabbage (page 73)
Salted Eggs (page 73)
Fried Lacey Eggs with Thai-style
Dressing (page 74)
Simple Stir-fried Greens (page 75)

MENU 8
An Easy Thai-Themed Party
(things you can prepare easily
ahead of time except for Som Tum)

Tom Kha Gai Chicken Coconut Soup (page 65)
Fried Lacey Eggs with Thai-style Dressing
(page 74)
Shrimp in Curry-Egg Sauce (page 66)
Moo Tod Fried Pork Cutlets (page 103)
Minced Fish Larb with Herbs (page 99)
Simple Stir-fried Greens (page 75)
Foolproof Som Tum Pla Rah (page 113)
Aunt Priew's Halo Halo (page 145)

MENU 9
A Meal I'd Eat Anytime

APPETIZERS
Yum Moo Yaw Pork Paté (page 117)
MAIN
Thai Sukiyaki (page 48)
DESSERT
Sankaya Fuk Tong Pumpkin Custard
(page 149)

MENU 10
New Year's on the Beach

APPETIZERS
Cashew Nuts Yum (page 79)
Nuea Dat Diew Salted Beef (page 78)
Pon Pla Tu Mackerel Salad (page 37)
Guaythiew Gai Maraa Chicken Noodle
Soup (page 44)
MAIN
Thai-style Chicken Biryani (page 138)
Thai Oxtail Soup (page 135)
DESSERT
Kanom Sai Gai Saffron-scented Jalebi
(page 147)
Kanom Pui Fai Cupcakes (page 150)
Coconut Ice Cream (page 151)

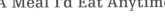

Preparing Thai Food at Home

In the olden days, Thai kitchens were outdoors, placed more than a few steps away from the main living quarters. Anyone who has inadvertently wandered past a cloud of holy basil stir-fry in the making knows the reason why. For Thai cooking to work, the aroma has to make your eyes water, make you cough, cling to your hair, linger on your clothes. This is probably why, even today, many Thai apartments saddle their kitchens with the worst views, because the assumption is the tenant won't be spending much time there. Unless, of course, they, like me and probably like you, are the types of masochists who want to cook Thai food.

At its heart, Thai food was meant to be a labor of love. *Kati* (coconut milk) was not poured out of a can or simply squeezed from a husk; the flesh had to be scraped from the inside with the help of a bench outfitted with a blade on the end called a *krathai* (rabbit coconut grater).

A cook sat astride the bench (unless she was a true lady, which meant she sat side-saddle because a lady must never spread her legs).

This bench helped her to efficiently scrape the inside of the coconut shell with the blade, a bowl placed underneath on the floor to catch the shredded flesh. The bits of flesh were then gathered in a cloth and squeezed; the first press yielded the *hua kati* (coconut "head," or cream). Water is then added to the second squeeze, yielding *hang kati*

(coconut "tail," or milk). Needless to say, it was arduous, time-consuming work. And that was just the one ingredient. Today, we are blessed to be able to buy our coconut milk at the market, or to shred our coconuts ourselves with the help of machines.

The All-important Spice Paste

Many of the spice ingredients in a Thai recipe are pounded into a paste—the foundation of Thai cuisine. Pastes form the base for soups and curries, chili dips, marinades, some stir-fries, and even some salad dressings. Commonly made with fresh herbs, they are the reason why Thai food boasts that extra oomph in flavor, unlike the heaviness of many other Asian cuisines. But to make those pastes, cooks need access to the number one tool in the Thai kitchen: the mortar and pestle.

Krok sak (mortar and pestle) are ancient cooking tools used in many cuisines. Thailand is no different. However, different sets accomplish different tasks. Mortars and pestles made of granite are good for pounding pastes for curries and chili pastes, but would bruise the delicate components of a *som tum* (grated salad) too much. For that dish, sets of wood, preferably carved from something aromatic like a mango tree, are the most prized. Like an old omelet pan, the more often a mortar and pestle is used, the more valuable it becomes.

Because the preparation of a traditional Thai meal was so time-consuming, residential streets and village pathways were alive with the sound of a rhythmic thwack-thwack-thwacking from the early afternoon onwards. It is even said that men chose their prospective brides by the loud, swift sounds that their mortars and pestles made as they worked, so important was the role that a Thai meal played to a family.

I have been told that Thai cooks can be gentle and smiley all they like, but that the kitchen is where all that pent-up aggression must

be allowed to run riot. I once read a profile of boxer Mike Tyson that said he hit his opponents, not just with the intention of winning, but to also cause harm. In this case—and only in this case—the Thai cook in the kitchen is Mike Tyson, mashing those paste ingredients into oblivion.

Eyes Beware

Of course, all that aggressive mashing will result in an unexpected problem once you start: protecting your eyes and face from flying chili debris. This is why many cooks prefer to fold a kitchen towel underneath the mortar to increase stability, and to keep the whole set-up from moving unexpectedly beneath you as you set to work. You can also obscure the part of the opening of the top with your other hand as you pound, like watching a horror movie through your fingers when it gets to a particularly suspenseful part.

Ultimately, you can never really protect yourself from the chili spray, apart from wearing glasses or putting on ski goggles. I am never thrilled when a bit of chili ricochets into my eye, but I have come to enjoy the tingly sensation the chili liquid leaves on the rest of my face; it's a bit like my nightly exfoliating toner. I like to imagine that, besides being delicious, chili liquid has similar skin-enhancing effects.

Now, you may be wondering to yourself, "Why can't I just use a blender and not have to worry about chili juice in my eye?" to which I would respond, "You to-

food (and David Thompson certainly is one) want to make their food properly, and that is not really achievable without a mortar and pestle.

Of course, one cannot have a Thai meal without rice. Yes, noodles have taken on a major part of Thai cuisine, but when it comes to the all-important evening meal, traditional Thais still consider rice as the most important part. In the olden days, rice was cooked in

tally can use a blender and not worry about chili juice in your eye." However, I firmly believe you would also miss out on many of the aromas that are released when you simply buzz everything up in a blender, where everything is chopped up very finely, but not mashed so that the essential oils are blended into the pulp.

The Krok and the Khao

The mortar and pestle are what ensure that not only does a delicious mash ensue from all your efforts, but that the mash will also smell the way it should—fantastically pungent. After all, there's a reason why David Thompson's restaurant Aksorn, which sports an open kitchen, resounds with the thumthum sound of various mortars and pestles at work while you are enjoying your meal. Sticklers for Thai

a large steamer set over a pot of boiling water. Happily for us, one of the great technological advances for the Thai home cook has been the *maw hoong khao* (rice cooker), which takes all of the guesswork out of making a nice bowl of *khao hom malee* (fluffy, aromatic jasmine rice). One only needs to make sure that the rice is not overcooked; jasmine rice grains tend to get ragged and blowsy at the edges like overgrown weeds when that has happened. But in the event you

are without a rice cooker, do not despair. At the end of this chapter, we will explore a sureproof, rice cooker-less way of cooking rice.

There are some types of rice that do not take well to the rice cooker. One of the most glaring examples is sticky rice, prevalent in the North and Northeast of the country. Instead, these cooks use a *huad*, a woven bamboo basket with a pinched bottom that fits over a wide metal cylinder with a big flaring lip, which is filled with a few inches of water and set over heat.

Get a Weave and a Wok

The slightly open weave allows the grains to be cooked, while still enabling them to breathe. It is imperative that they do not get too hard and sticky, but also not too mushy and gluey. Cooking sticky rice is actually a bit of a tightrope walk, involving more steps than you would expect. In the Northern Thai section, we will discover the best way to ensure perfectly glutinous rice, every time.

To keep that sticky rice in good shape at the table, you need a woven bamboo basket called a *gratib*, which has the same slightly open weave as the *huad*. This keeps the grains moist. Unlike white jasmine rice (*khao suay*, or "beautiful rice"), sticky rice can get hard when kept in a big bowl on the table, as the open air dries the grains out. The *gratib*, which has a cover, keeps the steam trapped; important because hard sticky rice grains can be unpleasant, especially if you are eating spicy food.

Another imperative of Thai cuisine is the stir-frying and frying that have become such a mainstay of the menu. *Grata* (woks), hat-shaped skillets with high sides that spread out from the base, are meant to withstand high heat and enable the easier tossing of the ingredients in the pan. Originally brought to Thailand by the Chinese, woks have now been incorporated as an integral piece of equipment in any Thai kitchen.

First-timers to wok cooking first need to clean their woks thoroughly before using them. This is because many manufacturers coat their woks with a protective oil to keep them from rusting when they are being shipped.

Next comes the seasoning of the wok. This helps your wok develop a natural non-stick quality, improving its performance each time you cook. To start the seasoning, heat the wok's surface over high heat, making sure to cover all areas of the surface (if you have wooden

handles, cover with foil so they don't burn). The metal might smoke and change color as you heat it, which lets you know that it's actually working. Once you're done, allow the wok to rest for about 15-30 minutes.

Next comes the moment when you have to oil your wok. Use an unscented oil with a high smoking point (like canola) and use a paper towel to smooth the oil over the inside and outside of your wok. Keep the layer thin. Then once again heat your wok, making sure to cover the surface and waiting until the oil stops smoking to finish the heating process. When you see the surface become matte, you have successfully seasoned that part of the wok.

Once you've finished, run your wok under hot water one more

time and clean the inside carefully without scraping off all of the seasoning you've done. Then, instead of wiping your wok dry with a dish towel, put it over the stove burner one more time to heat the wok in order to evaporate the water away. You can repeat the entire process one or two more times if you are the type of person who likes to do three reps of everything in the gym. Otherwise, you can now finally put your wok away or use it to make something. From now on, you will be washing your wok with hot water and a sponge (but not with a wire brush or soap).

Tools of the Trade

After the wok, the *meed* (knife) is the next important part of the Thai cook's arsenal. However, Thai chefs do not see their knives the same way that Western chefs do. In the West, chefs are in charge of their own knives, sharpening them, collecting them, making them ex-

tensions of the chefs themselves. In Thailand, knives are more of a communal thing, shared in the kitchen to use (or abuse) as that particular person sees fit. The theory behind this differing philosophy is that in the olden days, metal for knives was precious, saved for weapons of war. This is why Thai cooks—like many other Asian chefs—can make do with a single battered *eeto* (butcher's cleaver) if need be. Indeed, a cleaver can be used from chopping through bone-in pork parts to carving julienned pieces from a green papaya.

No Weapons at the Table

In spite of the tendency for Thai cooks to go through knives at a relatively rapid rate, they remain important tools in the kitchen. Food is always cut into bite-sized pieces before it is brought to the diner (there is a lack of personal cutting knives at the table, possibly because of the reason delineated above), thereby ensuring it is easy to eat with rice, spoon and fork. Because plates are communal and meals are family-style, bite-sized pieces also make it easy to share.

With knives assuming such im-

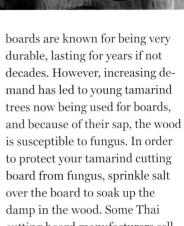

portance in the kitchen, *kieng* (cutting boards) are obviously prime considerations as well. For many cooks, the most prized cutting boards to obtain are those made of tamarind wood, which is considered so strong that Thai butcher's counter-tops are often made of it. Thais also believe they impart a tangy "flavor" to the ingredients cut on them and that fat and grease from the meats are eventually absorbed by the wood, making it stronger.

Tamarind trees are still abundant in Thailand because, in the olden days, Thais planted them wherever they went. Their fruit pods are eaten and their pulp incorporated into sauces and soups. Older trees that are not able to supply this fruit become prime candidates for the cutting board.

Because of their size, old trees can yield many boards. Those

boards are known for being very durable, lasting for years if not decades. However, increasing demand has led to young tamarind trees now being used for boards, and because of their sap, the wood is susceptible to fungus. In order to protect your tamarind cutting board from fungus, sprinkle salt over the board to soak up the damp in the wood. Some Thai cutting board manufacturers sell their boards already "pre-salted" or treated in brine.

Cooking with Steam

The last item that may prove indispensable to the Thai home cook is the *maw nung* (stainless steel steamer), used to cook everything from a whole fish in lime juice and chilies to a pumpkin stuffed with coconut custard. Steaming is one of the more important cooking methods in Thai cuisine, alongside grilling and frying, and is particularly useful for both seafood and desserts. Of course, people without a premium of kitchen space

can get around having a steamer by improvising one with a conical fine mesh strainer (what the French call a "chinois") set over a boiling pot of water (what with the mortar and pestle, cleaver and chopping block, you may have trouble finding any more space). However, if you have a steamer and not a *huad* or rice cooker, you can make do with cooking sticky rice in a steamer by laying cheesecloth over the holes over boiling water, or making jasmine rice by boiling it in a saucepan.

Naturally, you don't have to rush out and buy every single piece of equipment on this list. I hope I have written down some substitutions and adaptations you can make with existing equipment. The only kitchen gadgets that you absolutely must have to make Thai food are really the mortar and pestle, the knife and the cutting board—and it doesn't even have to be tamarind! Those two things, plus maybe a saucepan with a lid and strainer (accompanied by an "if there's a will there's a way" attitude) will ensure that anything you attempt in the kitchen, Thai-wise, is already 60 percent there.

How to Make Great Steamed Thai Rice

It seems like it would be a no-brainer, especially in the age of microwavable white rice, but Thai rice is special (says this Thai person) due to its fragrant aroma. Obviously, then, it's best to use *khao hom malee*, or white jasmine rice, preferably from Thailand. Barring that, though, you can really use any rice you prefer—riceberry, red rice, brown rice, you name it. As long as it's fluffy and not soggy, you're golden (although if it's super soggy, you can resort to making a Thai rice porridge. See page 72 for details).

First off, please wash your rice. This does not mean getting a good scrub on with your dishwashing sponge. Just submerge your rice grains in water in a nice deep pot and then scrunch your hands around a bit, trying to get to every bit of rice. Drain through a nice fine-meshed sieve and repeat the cleaning process. A good rule of thumb is to wash and drain the rice three times; some people say to wash the grains until the water runs clear, but that will take all day and we don't have that kind of time.

What will you need besides white jasmine rice? A soup pot, water and a stove. The typical ratio of rice to water is one cup rice to two cups of water, but what a lot of Thai cooks do is to fill the water until the level of the rice is under the level of the water by as much as the first knuckle of your middle finger. Make sure your pot is big enough to hold the rice as it cooks.

Bring your water to a boil and then reduce to a simmer. Cover and wait for about 15 minutes/cup of rice cooked. After then, check to see how your rice is doing and if the water is still there, re-cover and cook for another 2-5 minutes. Once the grains have absorbed all the water, leave it covered for a few more minutes, and then fluff with a fork before you're ready to serve.

Using Authentic Thai Ingredients

Here's an alphabetized rundown of the most common ingredients in Thai cooking that you are likely to encounter, and good substitutes for some of them if you can't get hold of the originals.

AMARANTH

ASIAN CHIVES

BAMBOO SHOOTS

Amaranth (*pak kom jeen*) is often sold in the West as a grain, but in Asia, it's a spinach-like leaf that is usually stir-fried or added to stews and soups. You'll find this in wet markets. Amaranth is cooked all over Asia; because of this, the most common form is known in Thailand as "Chinese spinach." The red-leafed version is known as *pak kom bai dang*, or "red-leafed spinach," while the type with thorns is *pak kom naam* ("thorny spinach"). Obviously, spinach and kale make great substitutes for this vegetable.

Asian Chives (*gui chai*) Also known as garlic chives or Chinese chives, this herb is taller and sturdier than Western chives, and is most commonly used in *pad Thai*. Although it would be preferable to use this ingredient when making,

your *pad Thai* noodles, you can always use Western chives in its place if you cannot find Chinese chives.

Bamboo shoots (*naw mai*) are commonly found in Northern, Northeastern, and Central Thai cuisines in soups and curries and as boiled accompaniments to various *nam prik* (chili dips). In the Isaan region, various delicious spicy-tart stews are made with this vegetable, but Isaan's most popular bamboo shoot dish is probably *soup naw mai*, a salad of shredded bamboo shoots served warm in a salty-tart dressing with mint.

Bananas (*gluay*) Thailand is lucky enough to be host to myriad variations of the banana, including the small, stumpy *gluay kai* (egg

banana) and petite, delicate *gluay leb mue nang* (lady finger banana). The banana that the West is most familiar with is the *gluay hom* (fragrant banana), but the one probably most prized in Thailand is *gluay nam wah* (Thai banana), which is sweet, starchy and suitable for a number of Thai desserts. The leaves of the *gluay nam wah* tree are also used to wrap up food before grilling them for chili dips. They are also used to wrap food before steaming.

Banana blossom (*hua plee*) The unripened blossom of the banana tree is also put to great use, as either a raw accompaniment to "greasy" dishes like *pad Thai*, or boiled and shredded in its own sweet-tart Central Thai salad, *yum hua ploo*. Because it can be quite

Basil When basil is mentioned, people naturally think of the Italians, but Thai food is also reliant on this herb. In fact, Thais rely so much on basil in their cuisine that they grow various different varieties locally. All the same, these leaves are rather fragile, so keep your basil in a cool but dry place. Once it turns black, you will have to toss it away. If you cannot find Thai types of basil in your market, go ahead and use the Italian kind for the smell. The three main types used in Thai cuisine are detailed below:

Holy basil (*bai krapao*) A thinner green leaf that lends itself to peppery or spicy dishes, adding a sweet, metallic undertow to the spice and a pungent aroma. The most famous Thai dish featuring this herb is, of course, Pad Krapao Basil Stir Fry, considered the unofficial national dish of Thai-

HOLY BASIL   LEMON BASIL   SWEET BASIL

land. Holy basil also features prominently in drunken noodles, *pad cha* (spicy wild ginger stir fry), and in some versions of *gang som* (sour curry).

Lemon basil (*bai mangrak*) This herb is considered sweeter than holy basil and gives off a pleasant, citrusy aroma. For this reason, it is most commonly used with seafood and in soups, as well as in a nice

steamed mussel or clam dish.

Sweet basil (*bai horapa*) Ubiquously referred to in the West as "Thai Basil." This herb is, as the name suggests, "sweet," with wide, bright green leaves. It figures prominently in one of Thailand's most famous dishes, *gang kiew waan* (green curry). It also serves nicely in a stir-fry, making it a nice variation on the usual *pad krapao.*

BANANA BLOSSOM

meaty and takes on other flavors well, Western cooks have started turning to this ingredient as a good substitute for meat or fish, hence

its emergence on some grocery store shelves. However, if you cannot find banana blossom at your local grocer, think of either canned young jackfruit or canned artichoke as substitutes.

Bean sprouts (*tua ngok*) Most commonly seen as the accompaniment to soup noodles or fried noodle dishes, bean sprouts when stir-fried in garlic is also a popular side dish to go with *khao thom* (rice porridge). You typically see bean sprouts with dishes that are considered "Chinese" like noodles and rice porridge.

BEAN SPROUTS

Bitter Melon (*mara*) Thais believe the older you get, the more you will appreciate this. I believe this must be true, because I now love it. This

Chilies (*prik*) Few ingredients are more intertwined with the identity of a country than chilies are with Thailand. Funnily enough, chilies did not grow in Thailand originally; they were brought to Thailand by the Portuguese, who carried them on their travels from Africa. Since then, Thais have wholeheartedly embraced this ingredient, and consider it a "health food" on par with ginseng and cordyceps.

Banana peppers (*prik yuak*) These relatively large (the length of your hand) peppers are a bright chartreuse color and boast a mild, slightly peppery taste. In the Central region, they are often sliced and stir-fried in Thai-Chinese dishes like chicken with cashew nuts, or pickled in vinegar to be sprinkled over noodles. They can also be stuffed with ground pork and encased in an egg netting

BANANA PEPPERS

BIRD'S EYE CHILIES

DRIED CHILIES

ROASTED CHILI PASTE

GOAT PEPPERS

as accompaniment to the popular Central dish "summertime rice."

Bird's eye chilies (*prik kii nuu*) Of all the chilies in Thailand, these are the ones most associated with its food. Named in Thai after mouse droppings, these chilies are formidably spicy and feature prominently in all regional cuisines. There are few Thai households that do not host one or two plants of their own; at every meal, they are either served fresh and whole on a plate or sliced and used to flavor fish sauce (*nam pla prik*). These keep well in the freezer.

Chili powder (*prik pon*) A staple on the soup noodle table, this is simply ground dried chilies. They are typically added to finished dishes at the table to increase heat.

Dried chilies (*prik hang*) When red chilies are dried, they become even more pungent and insistent in their spice level. In the North, they are used sparingly as garnishes to ground meat salads like *larb*. In the South, they are added to spice mixtures to amplify the spices that are already there, making that cuisine the spiciest in all the land.

Goat peppers (*prik chee fah*) Also known as spur or finger-length chilies, "red" or "green" chilies, they are larger than bird's eye chilies and feature pointed ends rather than the snub noses on the bird's eyes. They can be used in any recipe in place of bird's eye chilies and are generally considered milder in spice level.

Young Northern Thai chilies (*prik num*) Reminiscent of goat peppers, these are similar in length but of a brighter green color. Prevalent in Northern Thailand, they are roasted, peeled and pounded in a mortar and pestle to form *nam prik num* or roasted green chili dip.

Roasted chili paste (*nam prik pao*) This is a standard seasoning in Thai cuisine, sold in markets in every corner of the country. It is most commonly used as a seasoning at the table, added to dishes like one would add salt or pepper.

jade-colored (though sometimes it's porcelain white) wrinkly-skinned marrow is really delicious when stewed, and when raw or blanched, makes a great counterpoint to salty ingredients, paradoxically making them sweeter. Note: Sometimes it's called "bitter gourd" in recipes, but in most recipes I've seen, that's actually another melon (smaller and deep green with a pebbly skin) that's even more bitter (sometimes it's referred to as *mara kii nok* or "Thai bitter melon," as opposed to the bigger and mellower "Chinese bitter melon." We are only using the bigger bitter melon in these recipes).

Cabbage (*galumplee*) This vegetable did not originally grow in Thailand, but since its introduction to the country (probably via the Portuguese), Thais have taken to it as either a raw accompaniment to a spicy salad like *larb* or *som tum*, or stir-fried in fish sauce as part of a standard Central Thai meal.

Cardamom (*luk grawan*) This spice most likely came to Thai-

CELERY

land via its neighbor, India, or Malaysia to the South. It is used in much of the South, most notably in Muslim-Thai Southern dishes like massaman curry. There are different kinds of cardamom: the Thai kind is more delicate than its green Indian counterpart, which is easier to find in the West. If using the Indian kind, use slightly less and in recipes like massaman curry, which calls for a chili paste to be made, remove the seed from the exterior pod before using or the flavor will be a bit harsh.

Celery (*gunchai*) Unlike Western celery, Thai celery has a thin stalk and large leaves, making it very fragrant. It is commonly used as a seasoning to spicy Thai salads like *yum*, where it adds crunch and a grassy underpoint to all of the chilies, which offsets the spice. Of course, you can use Western celery in place of this ingredient. However, it won't be as fragrant.

Cinnamon (*ob choy*) This is not an ingredient many would associate with Thai cuisine, but it is used in some dishes, most notably in Northern Thai *larb*. However, it is not used in any Thai desserts.

Coconut (*maprao*) This is a native Thai ingredient that is still widely used even today (although not so much in Northern and Northeastern cooking). Coconut flesh is important in Thai desserts, and the young coconut itself is popular as a refreshing drink all over Thailand.

Coconut milk (*kati*) The milk of the coconut, much easier to ob-

COCONUT MILK

tain today than in the olden days, features in both sweet and savory dishes, particularly from the Central region. While fresh coconut milk is obviously best, most supermarkets now carry canned and/or UHT iterations of coconut milk. Thais often separate the "head" or thick cream of the coconut milk from the "tail" or watery coconut milk, adding them in different stages of the cooking process. Coconut cream is also used more widely in desserts, often as topping for sweet sticky rice.

Coconut shoots (*yod maprao*) The fresh young flesh of the green coconut can be added to soups like spicy lemongrass soup, or in stir-fries like drunken noodles. They can also be made into a spicy *yum* salad. If you cannot find coconut shoots, you may want to use canned hearts of palm instead.

Coriander leaves (*pak chee, aka cilantro*) This herb is either loved or hated by diners. Some liken its smell and taste to that of bedbugs; others associate the smell with greenery and freshness (I fall

CORIANDER ROOT

into this camp, of course). In any case, if you love coriander leaves, there really is no substitute for it. Just make sure not to confuse it with Italian parsley. No need to destem; both the leaves and stems, chopped, are used in Thai cooking.

Coriander root *(rak pak chee, aka cilantro root)* Again, this is coriander smell and flavor, concentrated. This ingredient is integral to many a Thai curry paste, chili dip or marinade. Of course, if you dislike coriander leaves, you will also dislike its root. If you do happen to like coriander leaves, make sure to save the roots in a Ziploc bag and store in a dry place in your refrigerator. Please keep in mind that the coriander roots sold outside of Thailand are quite small; if you are abroad, please use 2–3 roots for every root called for in the recipe. I'm told that in Europe, the roots are so flimsy as to be unusable; in that case, use stems mixed with leaves as a substitute.

Coriander seed *(luk pak chee)* Of course, coriander seeds are also used in curry pastes and marinades. As they are sold in the spice section, these can also be used as substitutes for coriander root if the roots you find are lacking.

Cucumber *(thang gua)* Out of all the vegetables in your garden, the humble cucumber may be the most useful for your Thai cooking explorations. Refreshing cucumber slices go with everything in Thai cuisine, from fried rice to *larb* to *som tum* to chili dips. Thais use them to counteract any spiciness; it's considered a better spice-buster than water.

Cumin seeds *(yee rah)* This spice, which probably came to Thailand from Malaysia, is used in many curry pastes, including green curry and massaman curry. It is always roasted and then pounded.

Curry powder *(pong garii)* No, it doesn't form part of a standard Thai curry paste. Instead, it is used

CURRY POWDER

in Thai-Chinese dishes like in *poo pad pong karii* (crabs stir-fried in curry sauce). In this book, we will be using shrimp (page 66) in place of crab for this iconic dish.

Dill *(pak chee lao)* This herb is used extensively in Northeastern cuisine as it imparts a fresh, "green" flavor to soups and stews. Unlike in the West, it is not used with seafood. Strangely enough, the Thai name for this herb translates roughly to "Lao cilantro," even though it is commonly used in the West.

Dried shrimp *(goong hang)* This ingredient can be ground up and added to salads and chili dips, or mixed in with the "Thai" version of *som tum*, considered sweeter and less pungent than the typical Isaan version of the grated salad.

Eggs *(kai)* Strangely enough, Thais used duck eggs more than chicken eggs in their cooking, and prize duck eggs over chicken eggs. Boiled eggs are common accompaniments to chili dips, salads and fried rice; they are not really hard-boiled, but cooked just until the yolk begins to set (called *yang ma-toom* in Thai, or "rubber tree sap"). Omelets are also a common feature on the Thai table, especially in the South, where they help soak up all the spice and gravy in the dishes. Texture plays an important role. Thai omelets are deep-fried, meant to be fluffy and a bit crispy on the outside. Ground pork is a popular ingredient in Thai omelet, but crabmeat can also be added when the cook wants to go a bit luxe.

THAI EGGPLANTS

Eggplants (*makuea*) Unlike the "long" purple variety, Thai eggplants are commonly round and crunchy, useful for their tannic qualities in combating spice. Raw, they are common accompaniments to chili dips; boiled, they play a role in salads and curries.

Pea eggplants (*makuea puong*) These tiny eggplants, sometimes mistaken for large green peppercorns, are used to combat spiciness. Their slight bitter flavor and crunch make them popular in green curries and shrimp paste chili dips.

Purple eggplants (*makuea yao*) A recent arrival to Thailand's shores, the purple eggplant is used mainly for the popular dish *yum makuea yao* (long eggplant salad), where it is grilled and served with ground pork and/or shrimp and slathered in a spicy-tart dressing and accompanied by boiled eggs.

Thai eggplants (*makuea proh*) Bigger than pea eggplant, these are either served raw with chili dips or boiled in green curries, jungle curries, or in their own salads, where they are commonly mashed to a pulp to make Makuea Mashed Eggplant Salad (page 111) and garnished with mint and roasted rice kernels.

Fermented soybean disc (*tua nao*) This fermented bean paste is sold in a dried disc form and is the base for many Northern Thai dishes. Substitute shrimp paste (*kapi*) if you cannot find *tua nao*.

Fish sauce (*nam pla*) Possibly the most popular ingredient in Thai cuisine, this condiment is said to have come to Thailand via either the Chinese or Arab traders. It is made of fermented fish and is used to flavor nearly every dish in the Thai culinary lexicon. Meals with rice are always accompanied by a small bowl of fish sauce, flavored with a few squirts of lime juice and studded with sliced chilies and garlic. However, be careful—this ingredient does expire. Once it turns black, throw it away. If you are vegetarian and cannot use fish sauce, substitute with soy sauce.

Galangal (*kha*) Unlike ginger, for which it is commonly mistaken,

GALANGAL

galangal bears a pinkish tinge near its "tail" and is considered cooling to Thais, instead of "heating" like ginger. It is used in many salads and soups, most notably *thom kha*, or the popular spicy-tart coconut milk-based soup. This keeps well in the freezer. If you absolutely cannot find galangal, you can substitute with ginger, but you must use less as ginger's flavor is much harsher.

Garlic (*gratiem*) Thai garlic cloves are smaller and more pungent than their Western counterparts, making them valuable ingredients if you can find them in the West. If you cannot, of course, larger Western garlic cloves will do but use slightly less than what is called for in the recipe as Western garlic is far bigger. **Beware** when using raw garlic for recipes—Western cloves will be far harsher.

Ghee (*nam mun gee*) This is, like in Indian cooking, clarified butter used in recipes that have an Indian or Middle Eastern influence. If you cannot find ghee in your supermarket, simply heat some butter and strain the fats (a sieve lined with cheesecloth works best). The clear liquid that remains is the ghee.

Ginger (*khing*) This came to Thailand via the Chinese and is prized for its "heating" abilities. New mothers are fed copious amounts of ginger in the belief that this helps to promote the production of breast milk. Ginger also figures in morning drinks, in Chinese-style stir-fries, and in popular Chinese-style desserts. You're likely to find it anywhere, but if you're really strapped, use ginger powder.

Hibiscus *(grajieb)* Also known in English as roselle, it is confusingly referred to in Thai as *grajieb*, which is also the Thai word for okra. However, this red flower is most commonly used in syrup for drinks and sweets and as natural food coloring for desserts.

Jasmine rice *(khao hom malee)* The most important ingredient in Thai cuisine, jasmine rice is synonymous with Thai "food." Old-fashioned Thais still believe that the evening meal, the most important meal of the day, must be centered around rice, not noodles.

Kaffir lime *(magrood)* These limes are pebbly on the outside, yielding little juice. The juice, however, is considered a good ingredient with which to wash one's hair. The rind, on the other hand, is an important seasoning in many curries and chili dips. If you cannot find kaffir limes, you can use regular limes.

HIBISCUS

KAFFIR LIME

However, the kaffir lime leaves, or *bai magrood*, are some of the most ubiquitous ingredients in Thai cooking. They are used in salads, curries, soups and stir-fries, and have no substitute. Most Asian supermarkets stock it. For this reason, buy a lot when you do see them, as they keep well in the freezer.

Lemongrass *(thakrai)* This has no real substitute and is widely used in Thai cooking. Aromatic and grassy, it is used in marinades, curry pastes, chili dips, salads and soups. The tough outer layers should be peeled away and only the thick lower third of the stem used. It's easiest to julienne it or use bruised larger bulbs that can then be fished out before eating. Lemongrass keeps well in the freezer, so buy a lot of it when you see it.

Limes *(manao)* This fruit is considered one of the ingredients that define Thai cuisine, adding its tartness to the brew that makes up the "salty-spicy-tart-sweet-bitter" flavor profile known all over the world. Thai cuisine only uses naturally sour ingredients and does

not incorporate vinegar, which is considered Chinese. The limes in Thailand are more like key limes, thinner-skinned with more juice. Alas, the larger, thicker-skinned Persian variety is the type more commonly sold in the U.S.

Mango *(mamuang)* When green, this can also be used as a "tartener," adding its sour flavor to the mix. Of course, everyone loves this fruit during the Thai "summer" (March–April), when the weather is at its hottest and juicy, orange mangoes fill the markets. The most popular type of mango is probably *nam dok mai*, which is juicy and has no filaments, but most Thais I've talked to prize the *ok krong* mango for its fragrant smell. **Green mango** *(mamuang kieo)* This type of mango is served green and has a tart, slightly sweet flavor that goes perfectly with salads, dressings for fried fish, or simply cut and dipped into a salty-sweet sauce (*nam pla wan*).

Noodles (*sen*) This ingredient came to Thailand courtesy of the Chinese, who began selling it by Bangkok's canals in the 1800s, giving rise to the country's first street food.

Egg noodles (*bamee*) These curly yellow noodles are adopted from the Chinese and resemble instant ramen in the pack.

Glass vermicelli (*woon sen*) Made of mung beans, these noodles are served in soups or in salads.

Rice noodles (*sen guay thiew, sen lek, sen yai, sen mee, sen chan*) Different iterations of these noodles—thin, thick, vermicelli, or rice stick—are used for either soup noodles or in fried noodle dishes like *pad Thai*.

EGG NOODLES

GLASS VERMICELLI

RICE NOODLES

PALM SUGAR

Pandanus leaves (*bai thuey*) Imparting a green, powdery aroma, these leaves are used in refreshing drinks, steaming rice, or in desserts where they are also used as natural food colorings, lending a fresh celadon hue to food.

PANDANUS LEAVES

Mint (*bai saranae*) This herb is mostly used in the Northeast, as a garnish for ground meat salads (Isaan-style *larb*) and *som tum*.

Ngiew blossoms (*dok ngiew*) In the recipe for Nam Ngiew Pork and Tomato Sauce Noodles (page 105), these dried blossoms are the central player, thanks to their chewy texture and slightly floral aroma. If you cannot find it, try to substitute with a chewy mushroom like shiitake cut into strips or enoki mushrooms thrown in at the last minute.

Orange, bitter (*som saa*) Old-fashioned Central Thai recipes make much use of the bitter orange, which is far more aromatic than

regular oranges. Because this is an ingredient hard to procure even in Thailand nowadays, you can substitute by combining orange juice and zest with lime juice and zest.

Palm sugar (*nam than peep*) One of Thailand's most important seasonings, this is considered more restrained and "rounder" in flavor than regular sugar. Of course, if you do not have palm sugar, regular sugar will do, but regular sugar is said to impart a harsher, sharper sweetness to a dish. Keep palm sugar in a cool, dry place. Since most palm sugar comes in disc form in Thailand, it must be shaved or grated for use in recipes.

Papaya (*malagaw*) This fruit grows in profusion in Thailand, but is perhaps most famously used while green in the Northeast as a major ingredient in Isaan grated salads, or *som tum*. In the South, both green and ripe papaya can be used in soups like *gang som*. Fresh ripe papaya is also considered a good antidote to constipation.

Peppercorns *(prik Thai awn)* Before chilies, green peppercorns were considered the original Thai spice. They are still important, featuring prominently in stir-fries like drunken noodles and in chili dips. When blackened, they are called *prik Thai*. If you cannot find green peppercorns in your grocery store, you can substitute black peppercorns.

Pineapple *(sopparot)* Another ingredient that grows in profusion in Thailand, the smaller, tart variety grown in the North and the sweet, larger type grown in the South are now cross-bred to form small, sweet, crunchy pineapples known as *phu-lae*, a highly prized variety in Bangkok. When eaten fresh, it is said to be good for digestion.

SAWTOOTH CORIANDER

Pomelo *(som o)* The season for this grapefruit-looking fruit is October–February. Unlike grapefruit, pomelo can be eaten in segments and has a slightly sweeter taste. Grapefruit can be used in its place.

Roasted rice kernels *(khao kua)* A common seasoning in the Northeast, rice kernels are roasted in the pan and then ground in a mortar and pestle. When sprinkled on a salad or meat, they add a smoky aroma and a nutty taste.

Sawtooth coriander *(pak chee farang)* Reminiscent of blades of grass, this herb boasts serrated edges and a sharp, fresh flavor that some say betrays a "soapy" character. Funnily enough, the Thai name for this herb is roughly translated to "Western coriander," even though few Westerners use it in their cooking.

Shallots *(hom dang)* As important an ingredient as garlic, Thai shallots are smaller and more fragrant than their Western counterparts. They are used in chili dips, marinades, curry pastes, and salads. If using Western shallots, use less

than what is called for in the recipe because Western shallots are far bigger. Raw shallots, if Western, should be used with caution.

Shrimp paste *(kapi)* The base ingredient in Central Thai cuisine, this is made of pulverized krill. The best variety is from Samut Sakhon, a coastal province south of Bangkok. Said to have come to Thailand via the Chinese, this ingredient provides a deep umami to any dish. Because it is hard to find a substitute, it's best to omit it and use fish sauce instead.

Soy sauce *(see ew)* This ingredient is Chinese, but is now used

POMELO

SOY SAUCE

in place of fish sauce in vegetarian and vegan recipes. You can also find it in many Chinese-Thai dishes like *pad see ew* (noodles stir-fried in soy sauce). Thais call the typical soy sauce *see ew khao*, which means "white soy sauce"; it's not white, but it's not the thick, sweet flavored sauce that is known as "dark soy sauce," "black soy sauce," or *see ew dum*. Needless to say, neither "white soy sauce" nor "black soy sauce" are the tamari soy sauce of Japanese origin, formed from the byproduct of miso paste.

Sticky rice *(khao niew)* The staple starch in Northern and Northeastern Thailand, this rice acts as a sort of edible utensil for both cuisines, which are eaten by hand.

Tamarind *(makaam)* This fruit, which is said to have somewhat of a laxative effect, is eaten as a snack, but the pulp is widely used in Thai cooking. Tart tamarind leaves are also used to flavor sour soups. Tamarind pulp comes in a hard block that you have to add to hot water to reconstitute the juice. Both of these keep well in the freezer. To make tamarind juice—a staple ingredient in Thai cooking—mix the pulp with some water. Mash with your fingers and strain to obtain the juice, discarding the pulp.

Thai anchovy *(pla rah)* This ingredient is ubiquitous in the Northeast. They are river fish mixed with sea salt, placed in a clay jar and allowed to ferment for weeks or even months. Use West-

TURMERIC

ern anchovies if you cannot find Thai anchovy.

Tomatoes *(makuea tet)* Perhaps because of their roundness, tomatoes have been given a similar name to eggplants, but that's where the similarity ends. A recent arrival to Thailand, tomatoes now feature in Northern Thai stews, Central Thai curries, and even *som tum*. The varieties grown in Thailand are not known for their sweetness and aroma, but farmers are making inroads on this issue, even reproducing some of the heirloom strains grown in the West.

Turmeric *(kamin chan)* This ingredient is used fresh, and is mostly used in curry pastes, although it also plays a role in Northern Thai sausage. When peeled by hand, it does tend to stain the fingers for a few days, as well as any equipment

you're using to process it. If fresh tamarind cannot be located, try the dry spice instead.

Wild ginger *(grachai)* Also known as "finger root," this herb has a fresh, bright flavor that makes it an ideal pairing with seafood. It features in curry pastes as well as in chili dips and stir-fries like *pad cha* ("numbingly spicy stir-fry").

WILD GINGER

Authentic Thai Dips and Sauces

Nam Pla Prik Fish Sauce with Chilies

This is the condiment that comes with every bowl of steamed rice set on a Thai table. It's basically fish sauce, flavored with lime juice, some raw garlic, and a number of sliced fresh bird's eye chilies (depending on your spice level). You can eyeball this, or follow the recipe below, which serves as a basic blueprint.

SERVES 1 ● PREP TIME: 5 MINUTES

3 tablespoons fish sauce per person
½ clove garlic, sliced
3–5 bird's eye chilies per person, sliced
½ tablespoon lime juice per person

In a bowl, mix the fish sauce, garlic, chilies and lime juice. Serve with a small spoon alongside a Thai meal with steamed jasmine rice.

Fish Sauce and Its Importance in Thai Cooking

There exists a certain kind of Thai person who believes that a dish isn't truly Thai unless it has fish sauce in it. This would make Thai vegetarian food, at its heart, an oxymoron. It would also make some local idiosyncrasies, like my family's fondness for Maggi Seasoning or my friends' preferences for salt, aggressive acts in culinary vandalism.

But some food experts beg to differ. Chef Bo Songivsava, of the critically lauded restaurant Err, says that the insistence on fish sauce as a major pillar of Thai cuisine is simply another example of the Central Thais placing their own food front and center.

"Fish sauce may have a significant flavor profile of Thai food, but there are so many dishes that are seasoned without fish sauce," she said. "Lots of Northern Thai dishes are based on salt and other salty seasonings such as *tua nao* (fermented soybean disc), *tao jiew* (fermented brown bean sauce) or *nam puu* (concentrated field crab juice). In both Northeastern and Northern Thailand, the fundamental seasoning is *pla rah* (fer-

mented Thai anchovies) while those in Southern Thailand is heavily based on shrimp paste and local soy sauce."

However, despite the myriad seasonings mentioned, no one can deny that fish sauce still plays a big part in Thai cuisine—especially if you are talking about Bangkok and the Central plains. When encountering a Thai recipe out in the wild, it is always best to arm oneself with a good bottle of fish sauce, just in case.

"We are not a huge fan of commercial fish sauces in general," said Chef Dylan Jones, the other half of Err. "However, there are a few brands that we fall back on when we are overseas, such as Megachef and Squid brand. Megachef is more fragrant and not overly salty like other commercial fish sauces; however, it is a little on the sweet side. Squid brand has a decent fragrance and is not too sweet."

Of course, Chefs Bo and Dylan brew their own sauces back home. Cooks interested in trying their fish sauce can go to Bo.lan Grocer's Facebook page at facebook.com/bolangrocer.

Sriracha Chili Sauce From Chef Black at Blackitch Artisan Kitchen

Chef Black is among a group of Thai culinary pioneers who call themselves "The F**king Chefs." Interesting name choice aside, they excel in foraging ingredients from local forests and crafting mind-bending dishes from them. The sauce outlined below is Chef Black's own recipe. Fruits like pineapple and mango may be blended into the sauce for an interesting and slightly sweet flavor twist.

YIELDS 2 CUPS (500 ML) ◦ PREP TIME: 15–20 MINS ONCE THE CHILIES HAVE FERMENTED FOR 3–5 DAYS

8 finger-length red chilies (Fresno, serrano or red jalapenos may be substituted)
8 large cloves garlic, peeled
2 tablespoons salt
1½ cups (375 ml) water
3 tablespoons shaved palm sugar, light brown sugar or honey (more to taste)
White vinegar, to taste

Mince the chilies and garlic in a food processor or crush them in a mortar with a pestle. Add the salt and mix well.

Place the chili mixture in a jar and cover with the water. Make sure to leave at least 1-inch (2.5 cm) headspace as the chilies may rise during fermentation. Leave in a dark corner for 3–5 days. Stir daily and make sure the water covers the chili mixture. This is to prevent spoilage.

Once the chilies are fermented, pour the contents into a pot and add the sugar and vinegar to taste. Bring to a quick boil. Reduce the heat and simmer for 5–10 minutes to reduce a bit and let the flavors meld.

Let cool a bit and then transfer to a food processor and blend until smooth. Store in the refrigerator.

The Real Story Behind Sriracha Chili Sauce

There once was a housewife in the town of Sriracha (near Bangkok) who sought to make a delicious sauce to go with the fresh seafood that arrived daily in abundance at her local markets. She aged the chilies, pickled the garlic and added sea salt and vinegar. The concoction that would later result would be named after the town in which it was invented. Sriracha Chili Sauce was born.

Or was it? Most of the world thinks of Sriracha as the tart spicy chili sauce bottled by Vietnamese-American success story David Tran of Huy Fong Foods. This sauce is now known worldwide and utilized in everything from chicken wing recipes to macaroni and cheese.

But the original sauce—a blend of spicy, salty, sour and sweet—is revered in its native Thailand, where it not only accompanies fresh seafood, but adorns stir-fried noodle specialties and deep-fried omelets (as ubiquitous on Thai tables as warm bread is on Europeans').

"Even in Thailand it's really a generic food (and a factory processed one, at that!)," wrote writer Philip Cornwel-Smith

of *Very Bangkok: In the City of the Senses*. Sriracha Chili Sauce in Thailand is "a bit like London gin, French fries (which are Belgian), Neapolitan pizza, Greek salad, or all those food styles like Bolognaise, Nicoise, Milanese, Linzer torte."

In fact, it is so intertwined with Thai culinary identity that its own origin myth is disputed. Of course, everyone lays claim to being related to the first housewife who created and bottled the sauce, but Sriracha Panich has actually written up its origin story on its company website (thaitheparos.com), putting it that much closer to true bragging rights. According to the website, housewife Thanom Chakkapak used only the finest goat peppers, aged for three months, and garlic pickled for exactly seven days. Although there are many local rivals in the Thai Sriracha Chili Sauce space, this is one that comes to mind when they think of that famous red condiment.

The Unique Thai-Chinese Approach to Seafood

Back in mid-century Bangkok, everyone knew that if you wanted a good seafood meal, all you had to do was venture to the Sam Yarn area of town, where a cluster of Thai-Chinese restaurants set next to the Sam Yarn market held sway. These restaurants, invariably run by the descendants of Chinese settlers to the city, featured a specific type of food that took fresh ingredients like fish, squid, crab and of course, chilies, and prepared them with Chinese techniques like steaming and deep-frying. Some of these restaurants, like Nakorn Pochana, still stand in the same locations where they were started decades ago.

But it took a breakout dish to preach the gospel of Thai-Chinese seafood to the rest of the world. Back in 1969, a humble San Yarn-area shophouse restaurant run by the couple Pichai and Chitra became the first to sell a crab dish in which fresh crab pieces were stir-fried in an egg-and-curry sauce. That dish, dubbed Poo Pad Pong Karii, is now known globally, served in restaurants worldwide. That restaurant, Somboon Seafood, now boasts eight branches dotted across Bangkok and has spawned enough imitators to give rise to a whole new category of Thai food, known as

"Thai-Chinese seafood."

You see, the combination of Thailand plus seafood seems like it would be a no-brainer, but aside from the South, seafood was not traditionally as beloved as it is now, with inland Thais preferring to dine on freshwater fish plucked from nearby rivers. With the popularity of a dish like the stir-fried crab in curry sauce, these Thai-Chinese seafood restaurants were able to bring their Chinese-influenced fusion dishes to a larger audience, introducing Thais to other favorites like whole fish steamed in lime and chilies.

Of course, the Thai approach to seafood also held sway over a big chunk of these menus, featuring simply grilled squid and shellfish over an open fire. And when it comes to grilled fish, it was the seafood dipping sauce that proved most important, turning a good, simple and fresh dish into something otherworldly. Like 100 different KFCs, every restaurant claims its own special, secret recipe, but the end result is generally the same: tart, salty, a little sweet, and a whole lot spicy.

Pravee's Seafood Dipping Sauce

Every Thai family can boast their own seafood dipping sauce recipe, and this one is ours. The most important ingredient, believe it or not, is the pickled garlic juice.

SERVES 4 ◦ PREP TIME: 10 MINUTES

2 cloves raw garlic, peeled
1 head pickled garlic (store-bought) with 2 teaspoons juice from the jar
5 bird's eye chilies, or to taste
1 large, or two small, coriander (cilantro) root
Juice of 1 lime
2 teaspoons fish sauce
½ teaspoon shaved palm sugar

Add the solid ingredients to a mortar and pestle and mash well, Thai-style, pounding like you have a grudge against the ingredients.

Gradually add the lime juice, fish sauce and palm sugar, mushing around like you are working at an ancient apothecary. Taste to adjust seasoning. Like most Thai food, this wasn't meant to lie around in wait for a few days. Use up as soon as you can!

My Dad's Seafood Sauce (Without Pickled Garlic)

But sometimes you'll encounter a person in the wild who just can't stomach pickled garlic juice from the jar. This recipe, from my father's table, is for them.

SERVES 4 ◦ PREP TIME: 10 MINUTES

15 small bird's eye chilies
5 cloves garlic, peeled
2 coriander (cilantro) root
3 tablespoons fish sauce
3 tablespoons lime juice
2 tablespoons sugar, preferably palm sugar

Grind the chilies, garlic and coriander root in a mortar. Once pulverized into a paste, add the fish sauce, lime juice and sugar, and keep blending until it forms a sauce-like consistency.

Jaew: The Quintessential Isaan Sauce

Like barbecue sauce is to the American South, *jaew* (or *jaeo*, whichever romanized spelling you prefer) is to the Thai Northeast. It's not obvious; Isaan food is, after all, known for its bright, uncompromising, fiery flavors; its aversion to sugar; and its dependence on *pla rah*, or Thai anchovy—none of which *jaew* has. But the sauce itself, perfect with grilled meats of every stripe (including very un-Thai-like submissions like lamb and rabbit), encompasses the real spirit of Isaan food: a heavy punch for minimal effort.

Now, everyone has their own version of this sauce, even if they don't originally hail from the Northeast. Such is the power of this sauce that anyone can come up with their own version, depending on how they skew, flavor-wise. It's a forgiving sauce and, once you get the hang of it, quick to make. The only things that one must absolutely have to get started are: dried red chilies, fish sauce, lime juice and ground toasted rice kernels.

The ground toasted rice kernels are arguably what will really make this sauce sing. They add a toasted aroma to the sauce that makes me think of home, while the taste is something like freshly popped corn. Unfortunately, the rice kernels are also the most fiddly bit of any recipe. Burn or scorch them in the pan, and you have to throw the whole thing out; the burnt smell infects the other kernels and muddies the entire batch with its bitter flavor.

To successfully roast your rice kernels, I'd recommend using a flat nonstick skillet. Spread an even layer of rice kernels in the skillet and roast them over a medium-high heat. Once the kernels start roasting, reduce the heat to medium. Keep an eye on them, tossing every few seconds so that nothing will scorch. While you're doing this, which can be very tedious, think PATIENCE. It should be done after you are done listening to three of your favorite songs, as long as none of them are by Boston.

When the rice gets to a light caramel color, or the hue of creamy peanut butter, it's done. Let them cool for a few minutes, and then get to work with a mortar and pestle (or in this case, technology does help in the form of a spice grinder). You are now ready to proceed with the rest of the recipe!

Jaew Chili Sauce

It was difficult for me to focus on one recipe for *jaew* to feature in this book, since there are so many other good versions. I finally asked my friends which they prefer, and they all chose my dad's. Enjoy!

SERVES 4 • PREP TIME: 10 MINUTES

2 tablespoons ground dried red chilies (mildly roasted)
1 tablespoon shaved palm sugar
1 tablespoon rice kernels, lightly roasted and ground (see above)
2 tablespoons fish sauce
1 tablespoon lime juice
2 tablespoons chopped coriander leaves (cilantro)
2 tablespoons sliced green onions (scallions)

Mix together in a small bowl the ground dried red chilies, palm sugar, ground roasted rice kernels and fish sauce. Stir until the palm sugar is fully melted. Add the lime juice and mix. Top with the coriander leaves and green onions before serving.

How Chilies Have Come to Define Thai Identity

"Thai food is not cookie cutter," said Tom Vitayakul, academic and owner of Ruen Urai restaurant in Bangkok. "Spiciness does not define Thai food. But people do seem to like it. The dishes that are well-known tend to have chilies."

Indeed. Out of all the culinary ingredients found in Thai cuisine, few are as inextricably linked with the national identity as chilies. Anyone who has watched a commercial for "Amazing Thailand" has surely seen a scene in which a hapless foreigner fans his or her mouth after taking a bite of spicy food, as Thais point and laugh at their distress. This is something that has become a part of a Thai person's view of himself or herself: the idea that spiciness = delicious = Thai.

The thing is, Thais have only been eating chilies for 400-some years, relatively recent in the history of a civilization established nearly a thousand years ago. Before then, local historians speculate that the food was likely to be characterized as *jued*, or bland, and possibly a bit salty.

Meanwhile, on the other side of the world, the first recorded instances of chilies being used in food were during the Aztec period in what is now Mexico. Those chilies, discovered in the New World by Spanish adventurer Christopher Columbus and his crew, were later brought back to Spain by one Peter Martyl, about whom little else is known.

From Spain, it was only a matter of time before those chilies would be taken up by fellow explorers and merchants and brought to other lands. It was Spain's neighbor, Portugal, who played an integral part in that spread.

"Chilies entered Thai cuisine thanks to the Portuguese trading network from South America," said Phil Cornwel-Smith, author of *Very Bangkok: In the City of the Senses*. "Previously, Thai spice had come from pepper, which is now distinguished as *prik Thai*. Chilies infused the cuisine not just in Siam—where they were the first Europeans to visit and found a mission—but also the foods in places the Portuguese colonized, like Goa in India, Sri Lanka and Malacca, the gateway to the Malay world. China's spiciest cuisine, Sichuan, is in the hinterland of Portuguese Macao."

Interestingly enough, Sichuan's recorded history of cooking with chilies has been estimated to be a little over 300 years old. But like Thailand, this region is now celebrated for its numbingly spicy cuisine. Like the Thais, the cooks of Sichuan were able to assimilate a foreign ingredient into their own food, creating something unique in the process.

"Thai people like to combine elements," said Ruen Urai's Tom. "They have an affinity for foreign things."

Thais called the new, foreign chilies *prik tet*, or "foreign pepper," as opposed to *prik Thai*, or peppercorns. They also became acquainted with *prik diiplii*, or "long pepper," a hot chili commonly used in Indian cuisine. Besides the ear-ringing POP that hot chilies lent to Thai food, cooks found that the chilies thrived in Thai soil, helped preserve food, encouraged diners to sweat (which paradoxically enabled them to cool off), and allowed Thais to scrimp on pricey proteins while loading up on rice to compensate for the spiciness.

Since then, chilies have become a foundational ingredient in Southern Thai soups, essential in Isaan dipping sauces and Northern Thai chili dips. In the "rice basket" that is the Central region, they are stuffed with pork and encased in deep-fried egg nets, tasked with seasoning coconut milk curries, chopped with garlic and plopped into fish sauce and lime juice. They are in just about any Thai dish that Westerners can think of, and found in dishes, like spaghetti bolognese and ramen, where the natives of those countries wish they wouldn't be.

"One can speculate why Thais like the fire of chilies, but to generalize, Thais choose strong sensory stimulation in countless other fields, whether in vivid colors, raucous sounds, pungent aromas, or painful massage," said Cornwel-Smith. "Chilies fit that temperament for heightened impact in everything."

As for the images of foreign tourists furiously fanning their mouths after bites of spicy food, Cornwel-Smith says it's really just about enjoying life. "It's a form of *sanuk* (fun)," he said. "And Thai food would be less *sanuk* without its foreign chilies."

Nam Prik Gapi Shrimp Paste Dip

People who are new to Thai food—and even people who aren't, including some Thai people—get turned off by the strong, funky smell of a good shrimp paste. For me, it's something that makes me hungry. I love a good shrimp paste dip, and consider it one of my favorite Thai dishes ever, even if, as a member of a Northern Thai family, I didn't grow up with this dish myself. Every Central Thai family probably has their own version of this dip. My husband's family does, too. This is their version, which includes a dash of orange juice and some bashed coriander root to add to the lovely aroma. Best of all, it keeps in the fridge for up to 4 days. The traditional accompaniments, besides fresh cucumbers and pea eggplants, are included below.

SERVES 4 ◦ TOTAL PREP TIME WITH EGGPLANT AND MEATBALLS: 45 MINUTES ◦ COOKING TIME: 20 MINUTES

1 tablespoon good-quality shrimp paste (*kapi*). The best is known as *kapi kuey*, made from fermented krill

3 finger-length chilies (*prik chee fah* if available, any color), sliced

10 small cloves garlic

5 bird's eye chilies, any color

3 coriander (cilantro) root

1 tablespoon shaved palm sugar

4 tablespoons lime juice

3 tablespoons orange juice

1 tablespoon fish sauce

1 tablespoon tamarind juice (page 29)

2 heaping tablespoons powdered or ground dried shrimp

For garnish: 1 handful of pea eggplants (optional), 2–3 Thai eggplants, 2–3 fresh cucumber spears, 2–3 peeled boiled eggs (cut into halves)

If you have access to banana leaves (but *nam wah* banana leaves only), please wrap your shrimp paste in a banana leaf and roast in the oven or grill over an open flame for 1–2 minutes. If not, roast the shrimp paste in a hot pan for 1–2 minutes until fragrant.

Mash the finger-length chilies and garlic together in a mortar and pestle. If you like it spicier, add the bird's eye chilies and mash them together. Otherwise, save those chilies for garnish at the end.

Add the coriander root. Pound to incorporate. Add the roasted shrimp paste to mix and mash to incorporate. Then add the palm sugar, lime juice and orange juice and mix together until well incorporated. Add the pea eggplants, if using. Lightly bruise and stir to mix.

Add the fish sauce and tamarind juice and mix. Taste for seasoning. It should be salty, spicy, sweet, and sour, in that order. Add the dried shrimp powder and mix. Taste and adjust seasoning if necessary.

Decant into a bowl and garnish with any bird's eye chilies that are left. Also garnish with pea eggplants, if you have them. Surround with fresh Thai eggplants, cucumbers and boiled eggs, along with Eggy Eggplant and Moo Gon Pork Meatballs (recipes on facing page).

Eggy Eggplant

Unscented oil, like canola
1 egg
Salt and pepper (to taste)
1 small purple eggplant (preferable Asian)
    sliced into 1-inch (2.5-cm) pieces and
    cut into ½ inch (1.25 cm) squares

Heat a pan over medium-high heat. When
the pan is hot, add the unscented oil.

Break the egg into a bowl and beat with
a fork. Season with the salt and pepper.

Take the eggplant squares and dip them
into the egg briefly before frying them in
the hot pan until cooked through. Continue until all pieces are fried. Set aside.

Moo Gon Pork Meatballs

1 lb (450 g) ground pork
1 teaspoon salt
2 teaspoons pepper
1 small clove garlic,
    minced
1 egg, beaten
Unscented oil, for frying

Mix the pork, salt, pepper,
garlic and egg together.
Form into small pork pat-
ties like tiny sliders. Fry in
a pan with hot unscented
oil until cooked through.

Pon Pla Tu Mackerel Salad

This recipe, when finished, looks a lot like tuna salad. However, it bears all the hallmarks of a good
Thai *nam prik*: assertively spicy, salty, tart flavors, paired well with plain vegetables and rice.

SERVES 2–4 ◦ PREP TIME: 25–35 MINUTES ◦ COOKING TIME: 10 MINUTES

10 Thai garlic cloves (preferably as they
    have better flavor) or 3–4 regular
    cloves garlic
6 Thai shallots (preferably as they have
    better flavor) or 4 regular shallots
3 finger-length green chilies (*prik chee
    fah*, if available)
5 small bird's eye chilies (deseeded if
    concerned about spiciness)
1 tablespoon fish sauce (if using a salty
    fish like herring, adjust down to
    taste)
2 tablespoons lime juice
1 small grilled deboned and shredded
    Thai mackerel. (Substitute any kind
    of mackerel or oily fish like herring,
    gemfish, sardines, bluefish etc.)
Coriander leaves (cilantro), for garnish
    (optional)
Sticky Rice (page 90), to serve

Roast in a skillet or oven the
garlic, shallots with skins
on, and both types of chilies. Please make sure to prick
the chilies with a fork or
they will explode. Roast until
blackened. When done, peel
the green chilies and cut into
thirds.

With a mortar and pestle,
pound the garlic and shallots
(remove the skins) into pieces,
and add the chilies gradually.
Add the fish sauce and lime
juice, and mix gently.

Add the shredded fish into
the dip with a spoon and
combine. Taste again and add

another squirt of lime juice if the
mix is not bright enough.

Serve garnished with the coriander leaves and accompanied by
Sticky Rice.

Nam Prik Kee Ga Dip

Nam Prik Kee Ga Dip is also called "Crow Poo Dip" because it resembles crow poo apparently. It is not pulverized very finely and is very chunky.

SERVES 2–4 ◦ PREP TIME: 25–30 ◦ COOKING TIME: 5 MINUTES

- 10 small (or 3–4 big) cloves garlic (smaller ones have better flavor and aroma)
- 6 small (or 4 big) shallots (same as above)
- 3 finger-length green chilies (*prik chee fah*, if available)
- 5 small bird's eye chilies (deseeded if concerned about spiciness)
- 1 tablespoon fish sauce
- 2 tablespoons lime juice
- 1 teaspoon shaved palm sugar (optional to mellow taste)
- ½ medium-sized cooked chicken breast

Roast the garlic, shallots and both types of chilies in a skillet or oven (or in a pan without oil). Please make sure to prick the chilies with a fork or they will explode. Roast until blackened. Peel the green chilies and cut into thirds.

With a mortar and pestle, pound the garlic and shallots (remove the skins) into pieces, and add the chilies gradually. Add the fish sauce and lime juice, and mix gently with the pestle. Taste, then add the palm sugar (up to 1 teaspoon) if the flavors is too aggressive.

Add the chicken breast, shredding it into the mortar, and then mix into the dip with a spoon. Taste again and add another squirt of lime juice if the mix is not bright enough.

Serve with sliced raw cucumber, coriander leaves, long beans, Thai eggplants and boiled eggs, plus salty beef and Sticky Rice (page 90) if you have it.

Nam Prik Tomato Chili Dip

This is 100 percent a "modern" dish, as tomatoes were not made into chili dips until relatively recently. However, this dip has a nicely mild, slightly sweet flavor that could convert diners who are queasy about spicy food. Note: Please do not use sweet ripe tomatoes for this recipe. Thai tomatoes tend to be flavorless, they are used more for their texture and hit of acidity than for their sweetness.

SERVE 4 ◦ PREP TIME: 20 MINUTES ◦ COOKING TIME: 10 MINUTES

- 3 medium-sized red tomatoes
- 5 finger-length red chilies (*prik chee fah*, if available)
- 4 small red shallots (Thai shallots preferred)
- 2 small cloves garlic (Thai garlic preferred)
- 2 tablespoons lime juice
- 1–2 teaspoons sugar, or to taste
- 2 heaping tablespoons powdered or ground dried shrimp
- 1 tablespoon fish sauce, or to taste (optional)
- Salt, to taste
- For garnish: (Fresh) cabbage leaves, Thai eggplants, cherry tomatoes, (blanched) bitter gourd, morning glory, pea eggplants, (grilled) catfish filets

Grill the tomatoes in the oven for 5–10 minutes until the skin is charred and the juices run. Peel off their skins and cut into small pieces. Set aside on a plate.

Next, roast the chilies until the skins are charred and they slip off easily, alongside the shallots and garlic cloves (also in their skins). They should be slightly charred but not burned. Strip the shallots and garlic cloves and set them aside with the chilies and tomatoes.

In a mortar and pestle, pound the chilies, shallots and garlic together until well mashed.

Add the tomatoes, lime juice, sugar and mix. Add the ground dried shrimp and adjust the seasoning if necessary.

Decant to a small container and surround with whatever garnishes are available to you. If you do not have all of the garnishes, do not fret. Just showing you what would normally be served with this dish in Thailand.

Crabmeat "Lon" Chili Dip

"Lon" is a funny thing. It's both a fiery chili dipping sauce and a sweet, unctuous dish leavened with coconut milk. Maybe these contradictions are why this particular dip is not often found on menus abroad. In either case, it's something of a staple on Central Thai tables, served at households for decades.

SERVES 4 ◦ PREP TIME 20 MINUTES ◦ COOKING TIME: 10 MINUTES

1 cup (250 ml) coconut milk
¼ lb (approx 100 g) ground pork
1 tablespoon finely chopped galangal
3 stalks lemongrass, tender inner part of bottom third only, finely sliced
¼ cup (25 g) finely sliced red shallots
3 tablespoons tamarind juice (page 29)
1 tablespoon shaved palm sugar
2½ tablespoons fish sauce
½ cup (100 g) fresh crabmeat
2 kaffir lime leaves, finely julienned
6 bird's eye chilies, red or green or both, bruised
2 finger-length green chilies (*prik chee fah*, if available), thinly sliced
Accompaniments: Cucumbers, winged bean, white cumin, cabbage leaves, Thai eggplants, pea eggplants

Over a medium flame, slowly heat the coconut milk, in a pan, until the surface ripples, then add the ground pork. When the pork is cooked through, add the galangal, lemongrass, shallots and season with the tamarind juice, sugar and fish sauce. Taste and adjust seasoning accordingly. It should be salty, sour and a little sweet.

Add the crabmeat, kaffir lime leaves, and chilies. Cook to a slight rolling boil again until the crabmeat is just cooked through, then turn off the heat. The consistency is hopefully not soupy, but more of a relish or dip. Put the relish in a small bowl, garnish with more bird's eye chilies if wanted, and surround with the fresh accompaniments.

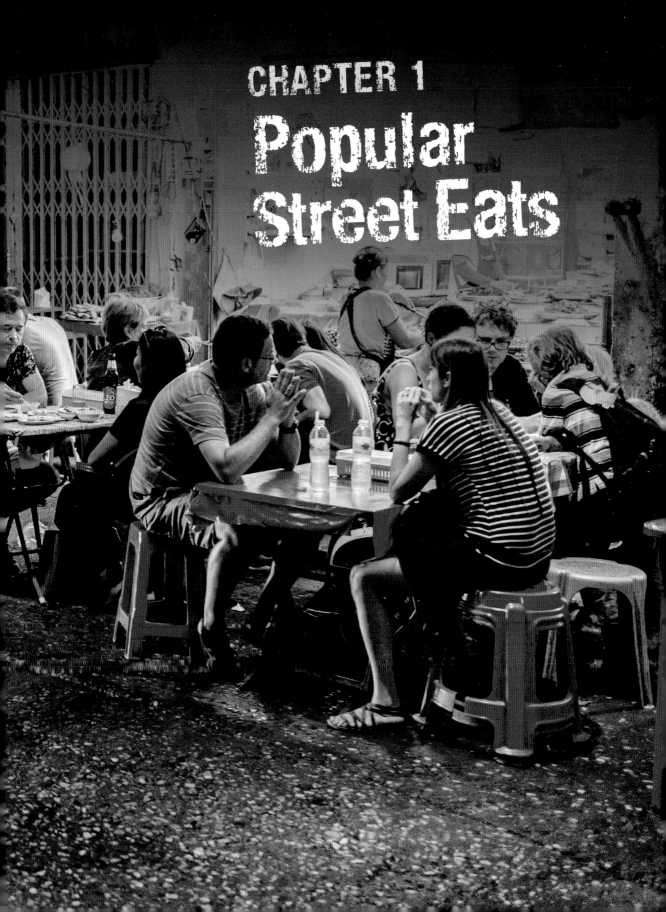

CHAPTER 1
Popular Street Eats

Where the Locals Eat
—on the Street

Few things are as linked to Thailand's image as closely as street food. Temples, beaches, diners watching a flaming wok at work as a Westerner furiously fans his mouth after a spicy bite: these are the things that come to mind when a trip to the Land of Smiles is on the cards.

But street food is not simply a cool way to spend the evening. Many Thais depend on street food, part of a delicate ecosystem that feeds low-wage workers and is in turn sustained by them. It is in this way that street food vendors help to prop up the backbone of the economy.

In the daytime, street vendors set up near shops and offices or in front of construction sites, offering the types of food—soup noodles, omelets, papaya salad, fried chicken—most likely to appeal to their target demographic. At night, a different vendor takes over, setting up shop near drinking establishments, dance clubs and snooker halls, offering grilled meats on a stick, egg noodles or rice porridge, ideal for ravenous drinkers in search of something to soak up all that alcohol. When it comes to street food, there is rarely a break; this intricate-yet-informal system runs on a 24-hour schedule that is known at heart by every Thai.

Street food is credited with allowing women to join the workforce en masse, by making it easy for them to pick up food for the family on their way home from the office. It has also given countless women a flexible and lucrative mode of employment that allows them to work their own hours and be their own bosses. Today, women like Michelin-starred Jay Fai, who labored for decades in obscurity behind flaming woks, have turned into bona fide celebrities thanks to Thailand's street food tradition.

Street food has also been a boon for immigrants to Thailand, particularly the Chinese. Barred from service in the more traditional money-making arenas of civil service or the army, the Chinese turned to street

food as a way to feed themselves. The industry they created has subsequently made fortunes for them in alarmingly short periods of time; the father of the businessman who created Beer Chang famously cooked oyster omelets in Chinatown, while the vendor who sold grilled pork on a stick outside the bars on Silom Road ended up driving a Mercedes to his street stall. Vendors have educated their children in England and the United States on the money they made from selling chestnuts door-to-door or frying noodles next to the road. In a world where the rags-to-riches story is becoming a rare phenomenon, Thai street food still found a way.

All the same, some Thais view the pairing of Thailand and street food with more than a little dismay. They want the image of Thailand to be more rever-

ent, more refined, more upscale. This has resulted in strange decisions like the attempt to clear major thoroughfares of street food while at the same time giving lip service to championing it and denying that a clean-up is happening at all. It is the subsequent, somewhat heavy-handedness of government attempts to control the street food scene that threatens to erase the chaotic charms that visitors to Thailand want to see, as squalid as they may seem to some of the locals.

At the end of the day, the sprawling disorderliness of Thai street food cannot be tamed; as the recent COVID pandemic showed, street food is a welcome source of sustenance when the economy is in a slump. In times of need, in times when you just want a good, quick bite, Thai street food will always be there.

Guaythiew Gai Maraa Chicken Noodle Soup

These are not the same chicken noodles with bitter melon that you normally find on the street; that version boasts lots of dark soy sauce and chili oil. What is good about this recipe is that it is EASY, and yields good flavor with minimal effort. That's what I like! What I also have come to like is bitter melon, which I hated as a child (I'm sure I wasn't alone). Thais consider it an ingredient for old people, and they are right—the older you get, the more you appreciate the bitter(ish), buttery flavors that bitter melon adds to the dish. Just make sure to blanch them before using.

SERVES 4 ◆ PREP TIME: 30 MINUTES ◆ COOKING TIME: 10 MINUTES

1 large coriander (cilantro) root, washed and coarsely chopped

1 inch (2.5 cm) galangal, coarsely chopped

1–3 small cloves garlic, peeled

2–4 bird's eye chilies

½ bitter melon, seeded, cut into half-moon sizes and blanched (chayote, green peppers, or zucchini may be substituted)

1–2 tablespoons vegetable oil

1 lb (400 g) chicken wings

3 cups (750 ml) chicken stock, or water with a chicken bouillon cube dissolved in it

4 oz (100 g) rice noodles

2–4 tablespoons fish sauce, depending on taste

1–2 teaspoons fresh ground white pepper, or to taste

Garnishes

Deep-fried chopped garlic

Coriander leaves (cilantro)

Green onions (scallions)

Vinegar with pickled chilies

With a mortar and pestle, make a chili paste out of the coriander root, galangal, garlic and chilies. Pound it into an even paste. Set aside.

Blanch the bitter melon by quickly pouring boiling water into a heat proof bowl with the prepared bitter melon pieces. Let sit for 20–30 seconds until the green color brightens. Drain and rinse the pieces under cold running water. Set aside.

In a soup pot or large wok, fry the paste in 1 tablespoon of oil until it gets a little color and becomes nicely aromatic. Add the chicken wings and cook until they put on a little color as well. Add another tablespoon of oil if the chicken starts sticking to the pot. Add the stock or water to the pot, cover and bring to a boil. Once it comes

to a gentle boil, add the bitter melon pieces and cook, covered, for about 8–10 minutes.

While the soup is cooking, cook your rice noodles according to the package instructions. Portion into individual serving bowls.

When the bitter melon has cooked (it's soft and the flavors have melded into the soup a bit), season the soup with 2 tablespoons fish sauce and the white pepper. Taste and see if more fish sauce is needed. (Optional): Once the soup cools, you can shred the chicken meat off the bones and reintroduce to the pot.

Ladle the chicken and soup over your noodles and enjoy with the **Garnishes**. Eat with chopsticks and a Chinese spoon like they do on the street.

Pad Krapao Basil Stir Fry

People like to think of *pad Thai* or green curry or spicy lemongrass soup as ubiquitous dishes in Thailand, but it's really holy basil stir-fry that millions of Thais eat every day, all over the country. With a juicy fried egg on top, it's considered the "quintessential Thai square meal"—quick, easy and delicious. Traditionally, *pad krapao* is seasoned only with fish sauce and palm sugar. Unfortunately, our palates have all been turned by delicious streetside vendors who liberally ply their stir-fries with soy sauce, dark soy sauce, and/or oyster sauce. This is not traditional, but it is yummy. This recipe (generously) feeds four, but I just managed to eat half by myself, so YMMV. After cutting all the vegetables, cooking time takes 3–5 minutes.

SERVES 4 • PREP TIME: 30 MINUTES • COOKING TIME: 5 MINUTES

3 large cloves garlic, peeled

5 bird's eye chilies, coarsely sliced (Thais typically use 10–12 chilies)

10 fresh green beans, sliced into ½-inch (1.25 cm) pieces and soaked in salted water

2 handfuls holy basil (*krapao*) leaves (the more you use, the more fragrant the dish. The wider "red" leaves are more fragrant than the "white" ones. Soak them in salted water so that they don't go dark in the pan).

1 large red bird's eye chili, sliced on the diagonal

2 tablespoons unscented oil for frying, 1 tablespoon at a time

2 cups (400 g) ground or cubed meat (I used cubed pork tenderloin because I like the meatiness of it, but ground meat takes on more of the delicious sauce)

1–2 tablespoons fish sauce (or soy sauce, whichever you prefer. I will not go so far as to encourage the use of oyster sauce here).

2 teaspoons dark soy sauce (for color)

1 teaspoon palm sugar

4 eggs

Nam Pla Prik (page 30), to serve

In a mortar and pestle, mash the garlic and chilies into a paste. Beware of flying chili seeds. Scrape out the mortar and set aside.

Drain the beans and basil leaves and set them in a bowl by the wok together with the sliced birds eye chilies.

Over medium-high heat, heat 1 tablespoon of the oil in a wok and fry the chili-garlic paste until fragrant. Add the meat and stir for a bit. Add the fish sauce, dark soy sauce and palm sugar. It should be quite saucy at this point. Taste and adjust the seasoning. Add more fish sauce or palm sugar if necessary. The taste should be salty and spicy but rounded with a bit of sugar. Add the beans and basil leaves. Give it a good stir, then turn off the heat.

In another pan, heat the remaining 1 tablespoon oil over medium-high heat and fry the eggs, one by one. The yolk should be runny and the edges should bubble up.

Serve *pad krapao* on a platter with steamed rice. Top with one fried egg.

Serve with the Nam Pla Prik on the side.

Grilled Beef Meatballs with Sweet Chili Sauce

One of my favorite street food spots is Luk Chin Anamai on Soonvijai Road, next to the hospital. I actually look forward to doctor visits because I know that I can go grab a bite at the noodle shop afterwards. While their beef noodles are very famous, this shop's meatballs are what I remember best. Unlike most diners who prefer ordering the finely milled, soft beef meatballs, I love the grilled tendon-y ones best and think this recipe replicates that texture well.

SERVES 4 ● PREP TIME: 30 MINUTES ● COOKING TIME: 10 MINUTES

2 cloves garlic, peeled

2 shallots, peeled

½ inch (12.5 mm) galangal, peeled

3 fresh kaffir lime leaves, stems removed and finely sliced

1 tablespoon shaved palm sugar or regular sugar

2 tablespoons potato starch

2 small bird's eye chilies

1 lb (approx 450 g) ground beef, the higher fat the better

1 egg

2 tablespoons fish sauce

2 tablespoons soy sauce

1 tablespoon peanut oil

Lime wedges and coriander leaves (cilantro), to serve

Thai Sweet Chili Sauce (optional)

Bamboo skewers

Thai Sweet Chili Sauce

4 finger-length red chilies or goat peppers (prik chee fah)

3–5 red bird's eye chilies, or to taste

6–8 cloves garlic, peeled, or to taste

¼ cup (65 ml) water

½ cup (100 g) shaved palm sugar or regular sugar

½ cup (125 ml) white vinegar

1 tablespoon fish sauce

Salt, to taste

1 tablespoon potato starch (cornstarch or tapioca starch may be substituted) dissolved in 3 tablespoons warm water

If using bamboo skewers make sure to soak them in water for a couple of hours before grilling.

Make the **Thai Sweet Chili Sauce**, if using, first so the flavors have time to develop. Put both types of chilies with the garlic in a mortar and pound with a pestle until a paste forms. Set aside.

Combine the water, sugar, vinegar, fish sauce and salt in a large saucepan. Add the chili and garlic mixture and simmer, over medium-high heat, until the sugar dissolves. Turn the heat to low and simmer for 5 more minutes to let the flavors develop.

Whisk in the starch mixture and gently simmer for a few more minutes. Remove from the heat, taste and adjust seasoning as needed. Transfer into a jar and let cool.

Puree all the dry meatball ingredients in a food processor until it forms a paste. Then add the meat, egg, fish sauce, soy sauce and peanut oil and blend until fully incorporated and slightly fluffy. The mixture will be soft and sticky.

Fill a medium-sized pot halfway with water and bring to a simmer. Wet your hands. Scoop a heaped tablespoon of meatball mixture and roll between your palms to form a ball approx 1½ inch (3.75 cm). Continue until all the meatball mixture is used up. Drop them into the simmering water, be careful not to spatter yourself. Poach for 2 minutes, remove them from the water with a slotted spoon. Set aside on a wire rack to drain.

When the meatballs are not too hot to handle, thread them onto skewers and grill. Serve with the lime wedges, coriander leaves and Thai Sweet Chili Sauce, if using.

Thai Sukiyaki

Unlike its namesake dish in Japan, a Thai-style sukiyaki meal is heavily reminiscent of Chinese steamboat, or hotpot. That makes it confusing for some visitors to Thailand expecting the Japanese meal of meat and vegetables cooked with a little water in a shallow central pan. It's also confusing for people ordering sukiyaki on the street—unlike the communal experience you would get at, say, MK in Thailand—the dish is brought to you already cooked in a bowl, either in a broth or dry. The important part of this dish, however, is the sauce.

SERVES 4 ● PREP TIME: 30 MINUTES ● COOKING TIME: 15 MINUTES

Make the **Sauce** by quickly blitzing the fermented tofu, pickled garlic and fresh garlic in a food processor or blender until well mixed together. Put the rest of the ingredients except the chilies and coriander leaves in a pan over low heat and simmer for about 10 minutes. After the ingredients have melded, add the chilies and coriander leaves and stir to incorporate. Adjust the seasoning to taste.

Make the **Suki** by heating the broth in a large pot. Add the glass vermicelli once it comes to a boil, then add the meat and vegetables. Wait until all the ingredients are cooked through (should take 3–5 minutes depending on ingredients), then divide them into four individual bowls, with or without the broth.

Accompany with small bowls of the **Sauce** and the **Garnishes** with which diners can choose to flavor their Sauce. If using eggs, break each egg into an individual small bowl to allow the diner to beat the egg. Some diners (especially Japanese) like to dip their meat in the raw egg and then in the Sauce before eating.

Suki

4 cups (1 l) broth of your choice, or water
6 oz (160 g) glass vermicelli
1 lb (450 g) meat of your choice (fish, beef, pork, chicken, shrimp, or a mix of all)
1 cup (100 g) chopped cabbage
Handful of each: shiitake mushrooms, firm tofu, spinach, baby corn, pumpkin, all cleaned and chopped

Sauce

4 cubes fermented tofu (preferably red) with some sauce from the jar, chopped
1 head pickled garlic (store-bought) with 1 tablespoon juice from the jar, chopped
6 cloves garlic, minced
1 cup (250 ml) Sriracha Chili Sauce (page 31)
¼ cup (65 ml) white vinegar
3 tablespoons soy sauce
3 tablespoons oyster sauce
1 tablespoon tomato sauce or ketchup
2 tablespoons sugar
¼ cup (65 ml) water
5–10 fresh bird's eye chilies, chopped
Handful of fresh coriander leaves (cilantro), minced

Garnishes

2 limes, cut into wedges
4–8 finger-length chilies (*prik chee fah*, if available), chopped
4 cloves fresh garlic, chopped
4 eggs, preferably organic (optional, beware of salmonella)

The Birth of the Irresistible Thai Hot Pot

Like all good things, the idea for Thai-style sukiyaki came to its creator in a dream.

The Thai-Chinese man, Towhua Saguai, was rewarded for falling asleep in church one day with the notion of adapting sukiyaki—a Japanese DIY "stew" of meat and vegetables flavored with a sweet-salty sauce and beaten raw egg—to Thai tastes. Taking a bit from the tradition of the Chinese hotpot, in which the food you want to eat is dipped into a communal broth, and sukiyaki, in which the sauce is heavily featured, Mr. Saguai crafted a no-brainer restaurant draw for Thais: cooperative and accompanied by an irresistible sauce.

The fruit of Mr. Saguai's dreams, the restaurant called Number One Suki, has since fallen by the wayside. But the genius of the sauce he thought up remains. Make no mistake: the sauce plays as important a role in the Thai sukiyaki dining experience as the tete-a-tete over the steaming pot of broth. A bewitching brew usually made of garlic, chilies, vinegar, coriander, and fermented tofu, the sauce in each Thai sukiyaki establishment differs slightly and is said to be a closely guarded secret.

A Thai sukiyaki meal is a simple affair. Yes, you can cook your own meal at the communal pot from the fresh meat, vegetables and noodles brought to your table. But if you are on the street, the cook will usually do the cooking for

you, serving your suki either in the broth or without (*hang*, or dry). In any case, the sauce is always present, whether you ask for it or not.

That sauce has led to big business. Since its birth in the 1950s, Thai-style sukiyaki has proliferated like wildfire across the country, resulting in big-business chain restaurants like Coca, which opened its doors in 1957 in Bangkok. Meanwhile, local sukiyaki chain champion MK claims over 200 outlets across Thailand and even a handful of restaurants in sukiyaki's birthplace, Japan.

Drunken Noodles

The common misconception is that "drunken noodles" have alcohol in them. But it's really named that way because it's supposed to be for people who are so drunk that they can't really taste anything unless the flavor has been pushed up to 11. TLDR: it's extra spicy and garlicky and is meant to wake you up like a bullhorn in your face … but much better than that, obviously. This recipe can be served with either rice noodles of any thickness or the everyday spaghetti in your pantry. Whatever you choose, it will be delicious. It's also important to have fresh green peppercorns for this recipe; it's just not the same without it. Less important but still nice to have: holy basil leaves, and shavings of wild ginger.

SERVES 4 ⚬ PREP TIME: 25 MINUTES ⚬ COOKING TIME: 5 MINUTES

10 oz (250 g) rice noodles or spaghetti
2 tablespoons vegetable oil
2 tablespoons green peppercorns
1–2 tablespoons sliced bird's eye chilies
2 tablespoons minced garlic
1 cup (250 g) shrimp, deveined
1 cup (200 g) squid rings, cleaned
3 tablespoons water, set to the side of the stove
½ cup (40 g) baby corn
2 tablespoons oyster sauce
1 tablespoon dark soy sauce
1 tablespoon light soy sauce
1 tablespoon fish sauce
1 tablespoon shaved palm sugar
½ teaspoon white vinegar
½ cup (15 g) holy basil leaves
1 tablespoon minced wild ginger (*grachai*), if you have it

Cook the noodles acording to the package instructions and set aside.

Heat a pan and add the oil. Heat the oil until smoking. Add the green peppercorns, chilies and garlic. Fry until the garlic is browned but not black. Add some water if the ingredients start sticking to the wok.

A big cloud of cough-inducing smoke might waft into your face; try your best to minimize your coughing fit.

Add the seafood. Wait until the shrimp turned pink and the squid gets more opaque before adding the noodles. Allow the edges to char, but not burn. If any burning is imminent, add a splash more water.

Then add the baby corn, oyster sauce, dark and light soy sauces, fish sauce and palm sugar. Stir to mix well.

Once the sauce is fully incorporated, add the vinegar, basil leaves and wild ginger (if available). Taste for seasoning. Stir for a few more seconds to wilt the basil leaves, and take off the heat. Serve immediately.

Pad Thai and the Birth of a National Identity Based on Noodles

Picture this: it's right after World War II and the country is recovering from time spent aiding the losing side. What was once known as "Siam" has now become "Thailand." To accompany the country's transformation to a constitutional monarchy, the powers that be desire the formation of a strong new national identity to go with it.

The winds of change that breed the rise of nationalism across Asia also blow across Thailand. Taking the lead of Prime Minister Phibun Songkhram, the government seeks to shore up its own Thai nationalist agenda by instituting a series of restrictions on the local Chinese, and other ethnic minorities: the eradication of regional dialects; no Chinese language signs allowed; even a ban on noodle shops near schools.

Not surprisingly, postwar Thailand was experiencing a recession, and the rice harvest had been appropriated by the Japanese, a lingering power in the region. This meant that Thais were to be more dependent on noodles—a Chinese ingredient—to fill empty stomachs. But how to eat noodles, the purveyors of which were almost uniformly Chinese, while bolstering a sense of one's own, fragile, new national identity?

This was the dilemma faced by government authorities in 1949. And the solution was surprisingly simple. They held a cooking contest, challenging competitors to come up with ways to turn a Chinese staple into something more "Thai." Thais at that time were learning to be Thai in other ways: in their behavior, in what they valued, in their education, in their dress. In a country that loves its food like Thailand, of course it was important to determine Thainess through what they ate.

The winning recipe took Chinese noodles and added Thai seasonings like palm sugar, tamarind juice, lime, with garnishes of banana blossom and starfruit. In another show of what Thainess really is, the award-winner was the wife of a government minister!

The tradition of the Thai government's active role in the "shaping" of the local cuisine was born. "There is often [government] interference [in food] because food is so symbolic to Thais," said Chef David Thompson. "There are two things the Thais attend to diligently: the stomach and the soul."

The original recipes for *pad Thai* (originally known as *guay thiew pad*, or fried noodles) are surprisingly simple. They either called for regular sugar and tamarind juice to be mixed into the noodles as they fried, or for a mixture of tamarind juice, palm sugar and fish sauce to be incorporated into the noodles after they're cooked. Soy sauce is never part of the equation: "That is only for *pad see ew* (stir-fried noodles in soy sauce)," says Chef Sujira "Aom" Pongmon, author of the *Baan Phadthai Cookbook*.

But what makes for a good *pad Thai* is less set in stone. "It comes from the quality of the ingredients and the sense of the cook," said Chef Aom, adding that it's not simply a matter of stir-frying the noodles. The cook must sense when the heat needs to be reduced, know how to impart a smoky aroma to the noodles, and how to keep the noodles separate and al dente yet glazed with sauce.

Because of Chef Aom's job with Baan Phadthai, she has traversed the width and length of the country seeking out the best versions, sussing out regional variations to put on her menus at home. In Eastern Thailand, versions incorporate blue crabmeat, crab stock and crab fat. In the North, the noodles are seasoned with black soy sauce and garlic.

In the end, the popularity of *pad Thai* both at home and abroad is easy enough to understand. "It's easy to eat and the price is not too high," said Chef Aom.

Pad Thai

This is probably the most well-known of Thailand's dishes. Although you may have your own favorite version of *pad Thai*, this one is fairly "authentic," by which I mean that it will be the most likely version that you would find in Thailand. This also means you won't find any soy sauce in the sauce.

SERVES 4 ● PREP TIME: 30–40 MINUTES ● COOKING TIME: 5 MINUTES

8 oz (226 g) *pad Thai* or similar dried, thin rice noodles

12 oz (340 g) large shrimp or protein of your choice (can be a mix)

2 tablespoons vegetable oil

4 large eggs, lightly beaten

2 green onions (scallions), thinly sliced

Pad Thai Sauce

2 tablespoons tamarind pulp

¼ cup (65 ml) hot water

½ cup (120 ml) Sriracha Chili Sauce (page 31), or store-bought (preferably Sriraja Panich or Shark brand)

3–4 tablespoons shaved palm sugar or loosely packed brown sugar, to taste

2 tablespoons fish sauce

2 teaspoon white vinegar

2 cloves garlic, coarsely chopped

2 pickled garlic cloves (store-bought), coarsely chopped

½ cup (120 ml) pickled garlic brine, from the jar

1–3 dried bird's eye chiles, stems removed, to taste

2 cups (470 ml) water

Garnishes

Chili powder (*prik pon*), to taste

½ cup (125g) roasted peanuts

2 cups (255 g) bean sprouts, blanched

1 lime (cut into wedges)

To make the **Pad Thai Sauce**: Put the tamarind pulp and hot water in a ramekin or small dish and set aside for 5 minutes. Squish the softened pulp between your fingers and discard any hard seeds, if necessary. Put the tamarind pulp and water, Sriracha Chili Sauce, palm or brown sugar, fish sauce, vinegar, chopped fresh and pickled garlic, pickled garlic brine and bird's eye chilies in a blender and puree until smooth.

Transfer the tamarind mixture to a medium saucepan, add the water. Bring to a low boil, and cook the sauce until thickened and reduced by about a third, stirring often, about 15 minutes. You should have about 2 cups of sauce.

Put the dried rice noodles in a large bowl and cover with lukewarm water (make sure the noodles are completely submerged). Soak the noodles until softened, about 30 minutes, then strain. Prepare your protein. If using shrimp, devein and remove the shells.

Heat a large wok or stainless steel sauté pan with tall sides over medium-high heat until very hot. Add the oil, let it heat up for a few seconds, then add the shrimp/protein of your choice and eggs and stir a few times to evenly distribute the eggs. Add the rice noodles and about a quarter of the Pad Thai Sauce and cook, stirring constantly, until the noodles soak up the sauce, about 30 seconds. If you are using a sauté pan, use tongs to gently help lift up the noodles and re-distribute them in the sauce, being careful to keep them in the pan. Continue adding the sauce, about a quarter at a time, until the noodles are al dente, 3 to 4 minutes. If the noodles are still firm, add 2 tablespoons of water and stir until they are softened.

Add the green onions, toss the noodles one more time, and transfer the *pad thai* to serving bowls. Sprinkle the chili powder and peanuts on top of each serving and divide the blanched bean sprouts among the bowls. Serve with lime wedges.

Tip Tamarind pulp is pure dried tamarind (unlike tamarind paste, which typically contains sweeteners). Thai pickled garlic is cured in a slightly sweet, vinegar-based brine. It is not the same as European style oil-packed pickled garlic.

Or Suan Oyster Omelet

This recipe is "wetter" than a typical *hoy tod* or shellfish omelet, which is crispy on the bottom and prominently features the seafood on top. This is more of a French-style scramble in which the eggs are barely set, topped with warmed-through but not fully-cooked oysters. It forms part of a meal with a side of steamed rice and can be topped with Sriracha Chili Sauce.

SERVES 4 ● PREP TIME: 10 MINUTES ● COOKING TIME: 5 MINUTES

1 teaspoon vegetable oil
6 eggs
1 cup (200g) fresh oysters
2 teaspoons fish sauce
2 green onions (scallions), chopped
Freshly ground black pepper

Heat a wok over high heat and add the oil. Break the eggs into a bowl and beat gently with a fork, seasoning with the fish sauce before adding to the hot wok.

Turn the heat to low, then cook the eggs until the bottom sets. Use a spoon or fork to fluff the egg mix slightly as you go while making sure you do not overcook or, even worse, blacken them. They should be a uniform bright yellow color.

Add the oysters to the top after the bottom forms, making sure to continue moving the eggs to ensure they don't overcook.

Once the eggs are cooked through and the oysters warmed, transfer to a plate and garnish with chopped green onions and black pepper. The eggs should be slightly runny.

The Hainanese Chefs Who Saved Siam from Colonization

To really understand the role of the Bangkok cookshop in Thai culinary culture, one needs to look into the history of the Chinese in Thailand itself. Fleeing from unrest in Southern China, the Chinese first came en masse to the country during the reign of Rama III (1824–1851). Unlike the native Siamese, the Chinese ate and congregated outside because their dwellings were too small. The idea for outdoor restaurants began to take hold.

The Chinese were known for their culinary prowess, able to cook anything asked of them. Little surprise, then, that Chinese cooks were keenly sought after by international households who could afford outside help, particularly since Thai cooks at that time could not make Western food. The best Chinese cooks were known to have come from Hainan.

Hence the first seeds of the cookshop were sown. During the reign of King Chulalongkorn, Siam faced pressure to modernize in the face of encroachments from colonial powers Britain and France. In order to stave off colonization, the kingdom would need to "prove" it was *siwalai*, the Thai term for "civilized." These efforts extended to food.

As a result, the official gala dinners at that time featured food cooked by Hainanese chefs who combined Western influences with Chinese cooking techniques (such as stir-frying) and ingredients (tapioca starch instead of flour). The dishes, which had to be served a la Russe, were brought to each diner on a tray by a server who could place the food on the diner's plate easily with one hand. Also, "steaks" and "chops" were ideal dishes for showing off one's Western-style prowess with a fork and knife. The food showcased Siam's *siwalai* approach to entertaining, playing a part in the kingdom's diplomatic efforts to portray itself as modern enough to stand on its own.

The chefs who honed their skills at Thai embassies and in wealthy kitchens opened their own restaurants in the mid-1900s, and would pass these recipes to their descendants. It is these recipes: the pork chop in gravy, salads in mayonnaise dressing, and *mee krob*, which would feature prominently in the cookshops that linger in Bangkok today. While these dishes are not what immediately comes to mind when Westerners think of Thai food, it is a cuisine that all Bangkokians know and have fond memories of: "It is the taste of my childhood," said Thai TV personality Chef McDang.

Mee Krob Sweet and Sour Rice Noodles

After all the writing I have done on cookshops, I have yet to find a good answer to why this deep-fried sweet and sour noodle dish was so popular in mid-century Thai-Western restaurants. All I can say is that every cookshop in Bangkok serves it. Unlike some of the versions found in high-end hotel restaurants, this cookshop version is made without tamarind and is softer and more rounded, with the sweet flavors mitigated by both saltiness and acidity. It's less sweet and tangy, more subtle. Think natural, subtle beachy waves instead of stiff helmet hair sprayed into oblivion.

One major rule: This must be cooked à la minute and served immediately. A good *mee krob* is crispy and crunchy, but not overly sticky or chewy like caramel. Sounds easy, but it's hard to do.

SERVES 4 ⏺ PREP TIME 35–40 MINUTES ⏺ COOKING TIME: 10 MINUTES

6 oz (160 g) rice vermicelli

2 tablespoons white vinegar

4 cups (1 l) unscented oil like canola

¼ cup (30 g) diced firm tofu

2 eggs

2 tablespoons diced red shallots

1 tablespoon minced garlic

1 tablespoon fermented brown bean sauce (*tao jiew*)

1 cup (200 g) protein of your choice or a mix of the following:

  ¼ cup (50 g) pork loin, diced into small pieces

  ¼ cup (65 g) fresh shrimp, diced into small pieces

  ¼ cup (50 g) chicken breast, diced into small pieces

  ¼ cup (50 g) crabmeat, boiled, shell picked out

2 tablespoons fish sauce, or to taste

2 tablespoons white vinegar, or to taste

2 tablespoons shaved palm sugar, or to taste

Fresh lime juice, to taste

Garnishes (optional)

Pickled garlic

Finger-length chilies (*prik chee fah*, if available), julienned

Bitter orange peel (*som saa*), julienned (optional)

Fresh coriander leaves (cilantro)

Raw bean sprouts

Slivered fresh limes

Garlic chives

Pre-soaked the vermicelli and the vinegar in some warm water until soft. The vinegar helps to make the noodles crispy. Dry the noodles completely by blotting with paper towels several times. Set aside and continue to air dry.

If you are short on time, the vermicelli can be fried without soaking and blotting dry. The soaked noodle version makes for a softer noodle that is more disc like than fluffy.

Heat a large pot or wok with 4 cups of oil until hot. Slowly add the dried noodles bit by bit into the hot oil. They should puff immediately. If not, let the oil get a bit hotter. Make sure the strands don't clump together as they cook. Fry the noodles in batches until puffed up and lightly golden. Place the fried noodles in a strainer or on paper towels to drain the oil.

Next fry the diced tofu until golden brown. Remove from the oil and set aside in a colander or paper towels to drain excess oil.

Carefully strain the remaining oil in the wok into a heatproof bowl. Reserve for later use.

Add 1 tablespoon of the reserved oil back into the wok to cook the eggs. Make sure the egg yolks are broken and scrambled. Once cooked, remove the eggs and set aside.

Add 1–2 tablespoons more of the reserved oil to the wok. Add the shallots and garlic and fry until aromatic. Add the brown bean sauce and protein of your choice (adding first the meat that needs the longest cooking time). Sauté until all the meat/protein are cooked through.

Add the fish sauce, vinegar and sugar. Taste and adjust the seasoning. Make sure it's not too salty! The sweet and sour tastes should come first.

Fry until dry or sticky. Turn off the heat. Add the cooked eggs, tofu and noodles and combine gently.

Serve immediately, garnishing with the pickled garlic, julienned chilies, coriander leaves and julienned bitter orange peel (*som saa*), if you have it. If not, give a quick spritz with lime for aroma. Traditionally Thais use *som saa* but it's not often grown abroad, so lime will do in a pinch. It's important that the dish has a lovely citrusy smell.

Top with raw bean sprouts, slivered fresh limes and garlic chives.

Khao Soy Curried Noodles: A Culinary Fusion Classic

Out of the many Thai dishes in the culinary lexicon, one of the bona fide "stars" of the past decade must be this Northern Thai curried noodle dish. At times referred to erroneously as "Chiang Mai laksa," this dish is actually a fusion of many different influences, all cherry-picked from cultures that have at one point or other called Northern Thailand home.

As a result, *khao soy* is one of the more interesting dishes in Thailand. Often mistaken for something Burmese (Wikipedia says the equivalent in Myanmar is called *ohn no khao swe*), it's actually a dish given to us by the Chin Haw, a Chinese group originally from Yunnan. This group (referred to as the "Haw" by Thais) gradually settled in parts of northern Thailand, bringing with them this delicious soupy mix of spice and starch. This may explain why *khao soy* always includes egg noodles, an ingredient considered exclusively Chinese.

Here's where it gets more murky. The Chin Haw were Islamicized Muslims. This would explain why the dish, if authentic, is sold in only beef or chicken versions in Northern Thailand. Yet strangely enough, the Yunnanese "Haw" attained a reputation in Thailand for bland food despite being credited with the invention of *khao soy*—perhaps

the yummiest bits of Chin Haw culinary know-how coalesced into the bowl of food that would become *khao soy*. Or, more likely, the local Thais wanted to malign the food of the newcomers.

Adding yet more fuel to the "I-don't-really-know-the-origin-story" fire, one particular purveyor, Lamduan Faham in Chiang Mai, claims to have come up with the dish all on its lonesome. The story told here is that the proprietor, the aforementioned Lamduan, made a bowl of pork (!) noodles for a group of Bangkok customers to which she added a quick dash of coconut milk at the end, knowing that Central Thais love their coconut milk. *Khao soy* (and a local culinary legend) was born.

To be fair, the version served at Lamduan—pork broth-based, lighter and more refreshing than the versions sold at Muslim stalls—may indeed have been invented by Ms. Lamduan on that very day. It's what came before (her version or the Muslim version?) that is ultimately the question here. In any case, both versions are topped with deep-fried crispy noodles and served with pickled greens, fresh shallots and slivered lime as garnishes, and both are just as delicious.

Khao Soy Curried Egg Noodles with Chicken

Out of all the dishes to come out of Thailand in recent years, this one may well be the most popular, found on menus all over the globe. Serve this when you need a pick-me-up (or even when you don't!).

SERVES 4 ◉ PREP TIME: 40 MINUTES ◉ COOKING TIME: 20 MINUTES

4 bundles egg noodles, ideally fresh
    (dried noodles are fine)
1 cup (250 ml) vegetable oil
1 tablespoon dark soy sauce
Chili Oil, to taste
1 lb (450 g) cubed chicken breast
2 cups (500 ml) coconut milk
3 tablespoons shaved palm sugar,
    or regular sugar
3 tablespoons soy sauce
1 teaspoon salt

Curry Sauce

½ cup (60 g) peeled and cubed ginger
1 cup (170 g) cubed Thai shallots (if
    using regular shallots reduce to
    ½ cup/85 g)
1 tablespoon vegetable oil
3 tablespoons yellow curry paste

Chili Oil

¼ cup (65 ml) vegetable oil
½ teaspoon chili powder (*prik pon*)

Garnishes

Deep-fried egg noodles (made from
    one bunch of fresh egg noodles)
3 green onions (scallions), sliced
1 bunch coriander leaves (cilantro),
    sliced
Chili Oil
Splash of fresh coconut cream
Pickled Cabbage (page 73)
Raw bean sprouts
Fresh chopped shallots
Fresh lime wedges
Sugar, to taste
Fish sauce, to taste
Chili powder (*prik pon*), to taste

To make the **Curry Sauce**, process the ginger and shallots in a blender or food processor, dampening with a few teaspoons of water until a thick paste is formed. Fry the mixture in the vegetable oil for a minute, then add the yellow curry paste. Stir-fry until fragrant, about 5 minutes. Set aside.

Make the **Chili Oil** by heating the oil in a pan and "sprout" the chili powder in the oil until it infuses the oil. Use some to season the noodles and set the rest aside as garnish.

Take 1 bunch of the egg noodles and deep-fry in hot vegetable oil until deep golden. Set aside and reserve for garnish.

Blanch the remaining noodles by placing each bundle in a strainer and immersing in boiling water. Stir with chopsticks for a minute, then plunge each bundle into iced water to stop the cooking process. Drain and season with dark soy sauce and Chili Oil. Adjust to taste. Transfer to individual bowls and set aside.

Put the chicken and Curry Sauce in a pan and sauté until the meat is just cooked through, approx 3–5 minutes. Add the coconut milk, ensuring a "soupy" consistency. Thin with water if necessary. Taste and season with the sugar,

soy sauce and salt. Pour this over the noodles and serve.

To serve, garnish with the deep-fried noodles, green onions, coriander leaves, Chili Oil and a splash of fresh coconut cream if you like.

Pickled Cabbage or fresh bean sprouts, shallots and wedges of lime go on the side. The diner can re-season the noodles with more sugar, fish sauce and chili powder also on the side.

CHAPTER 2
Bangkok and Central Thai Food

The Beating Heart of
Thailand's Cuisine

Fish sauce. Shrimp paste. Lemongrass. Galangal. Coconut milk. These are the ingredients that people think of when they think of Thai food. What they may not know is that these ingredients are really the building blocks of Central Thai cuisine, the elements needed to create the balancing act between sweet, salty, sour, and spicy that is so vaunted among global gourmets.

The central region, of which Bangkok is probably the most famous part, is considered the country's "rice basket," and the area where some of Thailand's most popular ingredients—limes, palm sugar, fish sauce, shrimp paste—find their most perfect expressions.

History has also added to the allure of Central Thai cuisine. Because Central Thailand has hosted two of the kingdom's capitals—Ayutthaya and Bangkok— the region has long acted as a sort of incubator for culinary ideas and influences, all of which stemmed from the royal palace. Emissaries from abroad, Thais returning home, and the best chefs that money could buy all combined to enrich a culture in which dining was considered part of diplomacy and networking.

But more than as an expression of its surroundings or a means to an end, Central Thai food spawns stories, a mythos around which the culture takes shape.

More than a few tales about old Thai recipes involve sitting at the knee of a beloved grandmother as she imparts her culinary wisdom, all the while thwacking ingredients with a mortar and pestle. These stories involve labor, and patience, and time: all luxuries in the current age of convenience.

Subphachittra Dinakara Sukarawan, known by friends as "Ja," has lived those stories herself. "Ever since I can remember, I have been cooking in the kitchen," says Ja, who now heads the MLP Institute of Thai Culinary Arts in Bangkok. "I started out helping my mother and grandmother, doing things like picking the leaves off the holy basil stems."

Ja is part of a family whose signature dish is *pla tu thom khem*, a Thai mackerel that is simmered for at least six hours so that even the bones are edible. It's also a family that boasts five different recipes for *kai*

jiew, or Thai-style deep-fried omelet, alone. They are serious about their cuisine. Yet time has taken a toll, even on Ja's family table.

"People used to be at home more, and women didn't work, so they had a lot of time to study the culinary arts and to spend time in the kitchen preparing meals," says Ja. "Because we knew our neighbors, we could exchange dishes and share culinary information. The education of food could then grow as a result. Today, our food is more about convenience."

Yet even in convenience Central Thailand is forging new avenues of its own. The boom of restaurants in Bangkok in the mid-1900s, spurred by Chinese immigration, spread to the rest of the country and brought the cuisine of families like Ja's to the public, in the process mixing it with influences from other corners of the globe to create something new. The region's restaurants became the new incubators for culinary innovation.

"You see a transition," said Chef David Thompson. "From eating at home to out, the democratization of food, there were generations of intermarriage and integration before it showed up on the menu."

Salmon Marinated in Nam Pla Fish Sauce

I struggled with what to use in place of fresh shrimp, which I think may not be easily accessible. I settled on sashimi-grade salmon, but any white, juicy, fatty fish will do: hamachi, lobster, or, yes, scallops. In a pinch, you can also use poached crab legs or even surimi. You eat the raw fish, which has been drizzled with sauce with the raw garlic and bitter melon slices. The garlic and melon actually make the fish taste sweeter. If your grocery store offers ready-sliced sashimi-grade fish, half of this recipe is already finished. If you cannot find ready-sliced fish, you slice it against the grain in half-inch-wide pieces or, if using lobster tail, slice it cross-wise (make sure your knife is very sharp).

SERVES 4 • PREP TIME 20 MINUTES

1 lb (approx 500 g) sashimi-grade salmon, hamachi, scallops, or lightly poached shrimp, lobster, crab legs or surimi

5–10 bird's eye chilies, finely sliced

1 tablespoon chopped Thai garlic or 1 teaspoon if using regular garlic

1 teaspoon chopped coriander (cilantro) root

2 tablespoons fish sauce

1 tablespoon sugar

3 tablespoons lime juice

1 small bitter melon, sliced and blanched

1 head Thai garlic, peeled, cloves finely sliced. If using regular garlic, use less and add to taste

1 handful mint leaves, shredded

In a bowl mix the chilies, chopped garlic and coriander root together. Add the fish sauce, sugar and lime juice. Taste for seasoning. Add more lime juice or sugar if necessary. Set the sauce aside.

Arrange a bed of sliced bitter melon on a plate. Place the sliced fish on top and the chopped raw garlic and mint leaves on top of the fish.

Pour the sauce over the fish and serve immediately.

Tom Kha Gai Chicken Coconut Soup

This dish probably needs no introduction. If you have been to a Thai restaurant before, chances are you've had it. The trick here is to use fresh galangal, not ginger.

SERVES 4 ● PREP TIME 15 MINUTES ● COOKING TIME: 15 MINUTES

2 cups (500 ml) coconut milk
½ cup (125 ml) chicken stock
1 stalk lemongrass, tender inner part of bottom third only, smashed and chopped
½ cup (50 g) finely sliced young galangal
2 kaffir lime leaves, torn
½ lb (250 g) chicken thigh, sliced into bite-sized pieces
1 cup (80 g) straw mushrooms (or any other type of mushroom)
1½–2 tablespoons fish sauce
1½–2 tablespoons lime juice
½ tablespoon sliced bird's eye chilies or finger-length chilies (*prik chee fah*, if available)
Handful coriander leaves (cilantro), chopped

Bring the coconut milk and stock to a boil, stir to combine. Add the lemongrass, galangal and kaffir lime leaves to infuse the broth.

Return to a boil and add the chicken thigh. When the chicken is cooked, add the mushrooms and bring back to a boil.

Season with the fish sauce, lime juice and chilies. Taste and adjust if necessary. Scoop into individual bowls, garnish with fresh coriander leaves and serve immediately.

Shrimp in Curry-egg Sauce

One of the most popular dishes in a Thai seafood restaurant is crabmeat stir-fried in a curry-egg sauce, said to be the invention of the Thai-Chinese couple who started Somboon Seafood. This one substitutes shrimp for crab, in case crabmeat is hard to come by.

SERVES: 4 ◦ PREP TIME: 30-40 MINUTES ◦ COOKING TIME: 10 MINUTES

2 lbs (1 kg) fresh shrimp
2–3 tablespoons vegetable oil, for frying
1 tablespoon minced garlic
½ white onion, chopped
1 tablespoon soy sauce
2 tablespoons oyster sauce
1 tablespoon sugar
1 teaspoon curry powder
1 teaspoon ground pepper
1 tablespoon roasted chili paste (*nam prik pao*)
3 tablespoons fish stock (½ cube fish or vegetable bouillon dissolved in 3 tablespoons water may be substituted)
1 egg

½ cup (125 ml) canned evaporated milk (unsweetened condensed milk). Coconut milk may be substituted if necessary.
3 finger-length red chilies (*prik chee fah*, if available)

Clean and devein the shrimp.

Heat the vegetable oil in a wok over medium heat and fry the garlic and onion. Add the shrimp and fry until just cooked through.

In a bowl, mix the soy sauce, oyster sauce, sugar, curry powder, ground pepper and roasted chili paste with the fish stock and add to the wok. Add the egg and incorporate throughout the shrimp.

Add the milk and chilies. Mix well and serve immediately.

Jay Fai's Tom Yum Goong Hot and Sour Soup

I've had this dish many times, but the best version I've ever had is the one cooked by Jay Fai at her now-Michelin-starred restaurant. Before the days of long queues and frantic diners, I had the chance to sit down with her after a meal and she told me she used a nice stock made of shrimp heads and a spoonful of oyster sauce. I've added that to the recipe here and it's great.

SERVES 4 • PREP TIME: 45 MINUTES • COOKING TIME: 40 MINUTES

5 cups (1.25 l) fish or chicken broth
1 teaspoon roasted chili paste (*nam prik pao*)
1 tablespoon oyster sauce
6 large slices galangal
5–7 kaffir lime leaves, leave some whole, finely julienne a couple
4 stalks lemongrass, tender inner part of bottom third only, bruised
4–8 red finger-length chilies or bird's eye chilies, bruised (this depends on your heat tolerance)
1 shallot, sliced
6 jumbo prawns with heads on, deveined (I find it easier to de-shell the prawn tails and to snap off the heads, which will be added to the broth)

5 tablespoons fish sauce
1 cup (200 g) oyster mushrooms, torn into bite-sized pieces
1 cup (155 g) young coconut shoots (substitute peeled green asparagus stalks or bamboo shoots)
Juice of 2 limes

Bring the broth to a boil. Stir in the roasted chili paste and oyster sauce. Add the galangal, kaffir lime leaves (both whole leaves and julienned), lemongrass, chilies and shallot. Allow to infuse for about 5 minutes, then bring to a simmer.

Add the shrimp heads, first scraping their contents into the soup. Wait 5 minutes, then season with the fish sauce. Add the mushrooms and coconut shoots (if using asparagus stalks, add in 20 minutes later).

Wait half an hour, or until the coconut shoots are tender. Skim the scum off the surface and discard the shrimp heads. Turn off the heat, then add the cleaned and deveined shrimp, and stir until the shrimp turn "pink."

Season with the fish sauce and lime juice. Taste and adjust seasoning accordingly. Serve immediately.

What is Kapi and Why is it So Revered?

Some culinary experts say it came from Burma or Indonesia. Others say it arrived courtesy of the Chinese. But what everyone would agree is that *kapi*, or shrimp paste, is one of the foundational ingredients forming the complex tapestry that is Central Thai food.

Much has been said about how Central Thai cuisine seeks to hit all of the flavors: sweet, sour, salty, bitter, spicy. For sweet, we have palm sugar, or in a pinch, regular sugar; acidity comes to us via naturally sour ingredients like limes and tamarind; bitterness and spicy, meanwhile, are delivered via various ingredients including bitter gourd and bird's eye chilies.

Saltiness is another story. Of course we use fish sauce; indeed, it's so important that some scholars swear that it's not Thai food unless fish sauce is included. But it's the pervasive funk of shrimp paste—recalling the depths of the ocean—that might comprise the essence of what Thai people think of when they think of Thai food.

Diners who are new to Thai food like to think of shrimp paste's aroma as, shall we say, less than ideal. But good shrimp paste, says Thai culinary instructor Subphachittra Dinakara Sukarawan, is actually *hom*, or fragrant.

"Good shrimp paste shouldn't smell bad," she insists. "It should smell really good, like something you want to eat."

Shrimp paste has been a part of Thai cuisine since time immemorial; the first mention of this ingredient are from tax invoices from the Rama I era. Make sure to avoid low-quality shrimp paste (in which baby shrimp eyes can be seen in the paste) as it can be scratchy on the throat going down. The best type comes from Samut Sakhon, or the Ranong/Nakhon Sri Thammarat area, where krill is abundant. If you cannot come to Thailand for shrimp paste, Sukarawan suggests trying the Tra Chang brand.

Moo Pad Kapi Stir-fried Pork

This is normally made with three-layer pork, but in the interests of our waistlines and health, Thais have started serving this dish with regular pork tenderloin. The dish is easy to make and popular as a picnic dish; the secret here is to make sure the shrimp paste is well cooked into the sauce before adding the pork, so that any bitter and/or fishy flavors are reduced. The flavor should ultimately be salty, with a slightly sweet aftertaste.

SERVES 4 ● PREP TIME: 25 MINUTES ● COOKING TIME: 10 MINUTES

3 tablespoons unscented oil like canola
3 shallots, julienned
3–4 finger-length red and green chilies or bird's eye chilies, (whole if bird's eye, sliced if larger)
½ tablespoon minced garlic
1 tablespoon shrimp paste (kapi)
1 tablespoon shaved palm sugar
5 tablespoons water
½ lb (300 g) pork, sliced
15 kaffir lime leaves, finely julienned

Heat the oil over medium heat, add the shallots, chilies and garlic. Stir fry until fragrant.

Add the shrimp paste and palm sugar. It will spit slightly as you combine it with the shallots, chilies and garlic. Create a paste. Add the water and incorporate well until a nice sauce is formed.

Only then should you add the pork, and cook until the pork is safe to eat but not hard.

If your sauce is not salty enough, add some salt to taste. If not sweet enough, add more palm sugar. Turn off the heat.

Serve immediately, garnished with the kaffir lime leaves, along with steamed rice.

Khao Kluk Kapi Shrimp Paste Fried Rice

This is a classic Central Thai recipe if there ever was one. Not only does it incorporate shrimp paste, but it also uses a jumble of different textures and flavors from across the spectrum to create something that is more than the sum of its admittedly already-great parts. It's a lot of preparation but the actual cooking is fairly simple. The final flavors are a melange of salty, sour, sweet and spicy. This recipe comes courtesy of my husband's great-uncle, Longlaliew Bunnag, formerly the head of food and beverage at the Royal Bangkok Sports Club.

SERVES 4 ● PREP TIME: 30 MINUTES ● COOKING TIME: 5 MINUTES

4 tablespoons unscented oil

2 tablespoons minced garlic

2 tablespoons good-quality shrimp paste (*kapi*), (Prachuab Khiri Khan province is best), roasted in aluminum foil or *nam wah* banana leave until fragrant

4 tablespoons lime juice

4 cups (700 g) warm cooked white rice

1½ cups (150 g) Sweet Soy Pork (page 71) cubed, or fried sweet Chinese sausage, sliced (approx 6 sausages)

½ cup (60 g) dried shrimp, ground into a powder

2 tablespoons thinly sliced shallots, reserve half for garnish

2 tablespoons sliced finger-length red or green chilies (*prik chee fah*, if available), reserve half for garnish

Fish sauce to taste

Garnishes

2 hard boiled eggs, chopped

Fresh coriander leaves (cilantro)

Green mango (optional)

Lime wedges (optional)

Nam Pla Prik (page 30)

Heat the oil in a pan, deep fry the garlic over medium heat until golden brown. Add the shrimp paste, lime juice, and any juice from the Sweet Soy Pork. Mix together until the shrimp paste is melted. Fold in the rice, Sweet Soy Pork or Chinese sausages and dried shrimp powder along with half of the sliced shallots and sliced chilies. Stir until well combined.

Taste and adjust the seasoning with fish sauce and/or more lime juice, if you like. Serve on a plate garnished with the remaining sliced shallots and sliced chilies.

Top with the chopped hard-boiled egg and coriander leaves. Served the green mango and lime wedges (if using) on the side. Accompany with Nam Pla Prik.

Sweet Soy Pork

If you live in Asia, sweet soy pork can be easily purchased at your local grocery store. If you don't, make this recipe, which should be a quick and easy way to cook a pork dish that everyone in the family will like.

SERVES 4 • PREP TIME 10–15 MINUTES • COOKING TIME: 10 MINUTES

2 tablespoons unscented oil
3 tablespoons thinly sliced shallots
¾ cup (180 g) shaved palm sugar (brown or white sugar may be substituted)
1½ tablespoons fish sauce
1 tablespoon dark soy sauce
1 tablespoon soy sauce
½ lb (225 g) pork loin cut into small pieces, roughly 1 inch by ½ inch (2.5 cm x 1.25 cm) thick
1–2 tablespoons water (only if sauce is dry)
Ground pepper, to taste

In a pan over medium heat add the

oil, then the shallots. Cook until opaque, then add the sugar, fish sauce and both soy sauces. Cook until the sugar melts and bubbles and caramelizes, around 5–10 min-

utes. Add the pork, fry until cooked through (no longer pink). If too dry, add the water. The sauce should be a little gooey. Serve immediately with a little ground pepper to taste.

Khao Thom Rice Porridge

Thai *khao thom* is often confused with *jok*, which is the Chinese-style congee, but *jok* is much smoother and more of a slurry. In *khao thom*, the rice grains are still recognizable. In Thailand, there are two general types of *khao thom*: the rice porridge with a broth base of whatever protein you are using (chicken, pork, fish, shrimp—but I never see beef) or the plain rice porridge with the little side dishes accompanying it. We usually call this type of rice porridge *khao thom gub*, or "rice porridge with side dishes," but it's also known as *khao thom gui*, or "Chinese worker's rice porridge," because it's a meal reminiscent of what Chinese workers used to eat while doing construction jobs in Bangkok.

SERVES 4 ⊕ **PREP TIME: 15 MINUTES** ⊕
COOKING TIME: 5 MINUTES (IF USING COOKED RICE), 40 MINUTES (IF NEED TO COOK RICE)

2 cups (450 g) uncooked
   jasmine rice
4 cups (1 l) water
Additional plain water to cover
Optional accompaniments:
   salted fish, Salted Eggs
   (page 73), fried garlic, green
   onion (scallion), coriander
   leaves (cilantro), sliced
   chilies, chili oil, fish sauce

If you need to cook the rice, first wash the rice in a large bowl in three changes of water, stirring the grains with your hand each time, or until the water runs clear. Cook in a rice cooker according to instructions on page 19.

After the rice is cooked, transfer the rice into a pot with enough water to cover. Bring to a boil again, over low heat, until the rice has "relaxed" into the water, stirring occasionally. It should become soupy and the grains soft and feathery at the edges. You can also use leftover rice for this porridge; in fact, that's probably the reason why this dish was invented.

Serve in bowls with suggested accompaniments.

Pickled Cabbage

Asian markets sell pickled cabbage in the jar or can. However, if you want to make your own, this is a relatively easy recipe. You can also do this with Chinese mustard greens. Pickled cabbage is a popular accompaniment to noodles like Khao Soy Curried Egg Noodles with Chicken (page 59).

SERVES 4 ◦ PREP TIME 24 HOURS PLUS 10 MINUTES PREP

1 small head Chinese or green cabbage (approx 1½ lbs/675 g), cleaned, cored and chopped into bite-sized pieces
2 cups (500 ml) + 1 cup (250 ml) water
2 tablespoons salt
Optional additives if you prefer a more flavorful pickle: garlic cloves, slices of peeled ginger, sliced bird's eye chilies

Wash the cabbage in a colander three times, draining each time.

In a large bowl, pour in 2 cups of water and add the salt. Add the cabbage. With your hands, "massage" the cabbage pieces in the salt water. Remove the cabbage from the brine and rinse under cold water to remove some of the salt.

Add 1 more cup of water to the brine to dilute. In a repurposed glass jar or bowl, place the cabbage pieces and any optional additives (if using) and the brine. Cover well.

Leave to ferment on the counter top for 24 hours. Taste, and if it's sour enough, it's ready. If not, leave it for another day. Store in the refrigerator until ready to use.

Salted Eggs

No *khao thom gub* meal is complete without a salted egg. Usually these eggs are covered in slivered shallots and chilies and doused in a fish sauce-lime juice concoction, but they are also good on their own, with just the plain rice porridge for company. Thais typically make these with duck eggs, but chicken eggs will do.

SERVES 4 ◦ PREP TIME: 1 MONTH PLUS 10 MINUTES PREP

4 eggs
1 cup (100 g) salt
2 cups (500 ml) water

Rinse the eggs and put them in a repurposed glass jar or glass bowl with a well-fitting lid.

Combine the salt with the water and bring to a boil in a pan, stirring. Boil well until salt crystals form on the pot's side. Once that has happened, turn off the heat and allow to cool. Pour the cooled salt brine over the eggs. The eggs need to be completely submerged under the surface of the water. Leave on the counter top for one month. If in the USA and using non home hatched eggs, refrigerate during brining.

When ready to use, hard boil the eggs, peel and serve.

Fried Lacey Eggs with Thai-style Dressing

Almost everyone knows how to fry an egg, but Thai eggs are crispy and frilled at the edges like lace. That is because the oil they are cooking in is very hot. The sauce is a typical *yum* salad dressing.

SERVES 4 • PREP TIME: 15 MINUTES • COOKING TIME: 5 MINUTES

4 tablespoons unscented cooking oil

4 eggs

Thai Dressing

4 tablespoons fish sauce
6 tablespoons lime juice
1 tablespoon shaved palm sugar or white sugar
2–4 bird's eye chilies, finely sliced, or to taste

Garnishes

Handful of fresh coriander leaves (cilantro)
1 small shallot, thinly sliced

1–2 small cloves garlic, thinly sliced
2–4 bird's eye chilies, sliced
A grind or two of cracked black peppercorns, or to taste

Heat a large pan until a drop of water sizzles on the surface. Add the oil. Carefully crack the eggs, one by one or two by two (depending on the size of the pan). Don't crowd. The edges should bubble up like froth on the edge of the ocean. Thais typically leave their yolks runny but you can cook yours through. When the eggs are cooked, set aside on a plate covered with a paper towel to drain the oil.

Make the **Thai Dressing** by combining all the ingredients in a bowl. Stir until the sugar is dissolved.

Carefully place the eggs on a serving dish and pour the dressing over. Garnish with fresh coriander leaves, thinly sliced shallots and garlic, chilies and fresh cracked black peppercorns, to taste.

Simple Stir-fried Greens

Another standby of the *khao thom gub* meal is the stir-fried green dish. You can use anything leafy, but for tradition's sake, we are using morning glory. Thai morning glory has thinner stems and bigger leaves than the Chinese version, but obviously the Chinese kind also works well. Other good options are pumpkin shoots, bok choy, Swiss chard, pea or sunflower sprouts, kale, and of course, spinach.

SERVES 4 ⬥ PREP TIME 10 MINUTES ⬥ COOKING TIME: 5 MINUTES

2 tablespoons unscented cooking oil
1 lb (500 g) green leafy vegetables (even lettuce works), washed well
5–6 small cloves garlic, peeled and chopped
2 tablespoons fermented brown bean sauce (*tao jiew*)
2 teaspoons white pepper

Once again, make sure that the pan is piping hot before you add the cooking oil.

In hot cooking oil, add the greens and garlic at the same time. Let the greens wilt a bit before adding the brown bean sauce and stir well to cover. After the greens have softened considerably and the sauce has coated them well enough, they are ready. Sprinkle with white pepper and serve immediately.

If you don't want to use oil in your stir-fried greens, you can use this method I learned from Panisha Chan of the "Thai Plant Based Recipes" group on Facebook. Ready your brown bean sauce on the side. In a hot non-stick pan, put some water or stock to cover the bottom. Once it starts boiling, add the garlic, and then the sauce that you set on the side. Once they all start boiling again, add the vegetables and stir until the vegetables wilt. Turn off the stove and serve immediately on a plate.

Thailand's Fast-developing Drinking Culture

It might be hard to believe, given that Thailand is Asia's third-heaviest drinking country after South Korea and Vietnam, but the country doesn't really have a food drinking culture. Not one that pairs drinks specifically with food, in any case. In fact, if local food experts like Chef McDang are to be believed, no wine really goes with Thai food. That is because Thais simply drink to get drunk.

At nice meals, Thais drink water, fruit juices, or iced coffees or teas. But when it comes to partying, Thais can light it up with the best of them. Case in point: the existence of *lao khao*, literally "white spirits" or moonshine, a rice liquor regularly brewed by rural Thais during times of celebration.

Lao khao is commonly called "Thai whisky" in English, but the term is a misnomer, using the name for a "high-class" liquor in place of what the drink actually is—dark rum. This explains why "Thai whisky" is so strong (regularly clocking in at around 35 percent alcohol), and frequently paired with mixers like soda. It's little wonder, then, that Bangkokians have gotten into the habit of watering down

their glasses of Johnny Walker Black with Coke or Fanta.

While these drinks aren't mixed to blend well with Thai food, particular dishes have sprung up around these drinks to form a whole new genre of local cuisine: *aharn gup gla-em,* or Thai drinking food. As a result, a whole new drinking culture has been born in reverse, around the drinks originally created by rural communities which migrated to the big cities via rural workers.

"It's not uncommon to see a group of colleagues walking into a restaurant with a bottle of whisky tucked under their arm, even during lunch," said Andy Ricker, chef and author of *The Drinking Food of Thailand.* "Mostly moderation is practiced with a cocktail consisting of as little as one capful of whisky poured over ice and topped with soda, cola, water or a combination of all three."

At the same time, Thailand appears to view its local alcohol industry with much ambivalence. Beer titan "Thai Beverage," maker of Beer Chang, wasn't even allowed to list on the Thai stock exchange. "Thailand is a Buddhist culture and drinking is generally frowned upon

by polite, pious society," said Ricker. "Most of the ruling class falls into this category, so drinking is often thought of as a low pursuit by those who hold power."

Lao khao is not the only drink that forms the centerpiece for a Thai celebration. *Sato*, made from rice, is frequently described as a type of "beer" due to its relatively sedate 8 percent alcohol content. And *ya dong*, made from *lao khao*, contains infusions of different herbs and spices meant to help with a range of ailments from period cramps to impotence. Streetside stalls selling *ya dong* can be found at any time of day, throughout Chinatown in the dead of night and at wet markets at the crack of dawn, also selling pickled mangoes and Thai water olives to mitigate the sharp sting of the liquor.

Helping to coax the trend of locally brewed spirits along is the exorbitant tax on imported alcohol—up to 150 percent. A Thai craft beer boom led to a flurry of local beer bars, as well as the creation of locally brewed gin, vodka and rum made from bananas, corn, sugarcane and rice.

Naturally, attention has now shifted to the drinking snacks accompanying these carefully crafted beverages.

Ricker, whose favorite drinks with Thai food are beer on ice and whisky soda, favors a cashew nut *yum* and deep-fried chicken tendons as his drinking snacks. But really, the sky's the limit when it comes to Thai drinking food: "Anything spicy, salty, sour, crunchy, chewy and/or herbaceous will do the trick!"

Nuea Dat Diew Salted Beef

A common drinking food with beer or Thai moonshine. A lot of times people eat it with sticky rice and a *nam prik*. It's also eaten by workers in the rice paddies because it's portable and keeps for a while. You need a dehydrator for it, though. Otherwise the meat is laid out in the sun to dry. Other than that, it's really easy!

**SERVES 2 OR 4 (IF EATEN WITH STICKY RICE) ● PREP TIME: 10 MINUTES ●
COOKING TIME: 5 MINUTES ● TOTAL TIME UNTIL READY TO SERVE: 3–4 HOURS**

1 lb (½ kg) beef sirloin tip (Thais calls it "coconut skin" beef because it's striated with fat)

3 tablespoons fish sauce (try to use Tiparos or Tra Chang brands, or a less sweet fish sauce)

½ tablespoon shaved palm sugar

½ teaspoon salt

1 tablespoon black peppercorns, or a healthy grind to taste

Slice the meat into ½ inch (12.5 mm), strips. Pound the meat on a cutting board with the flat side of a meat tenderizer to break apart the strands a bit. Mix in all the ingredients and marinate for 2–3 hours in the refrigerator.

Set the dehydrator or oven to 70°F (21°C), lay out the meat so that the pieces do not touch or overlap. Slow cook for 60 minutes. After half an hour, dab away any liquid underneath each piece with a tissue and cook for another half an hour.

Beef can be kept in the freezer until ready to eat. Otherwise, fry in 2–3 tablespoons of unscented oil over medium heat and taste the first few pieces. If not salty enough, marinate the rest of the pieces in fish sauce only for 5 minutes before frying the rest. Serve with Sticky Rice (page 90) or steamed white rice with Nam Pla Prik (page 30).

Cashew Nuts Yum

A variation of this spicy nut salad is served wherever there is alcohol on the menu. Our version includes deep-fried kaffir lime leaves and lime, but if you don't want to use them, it's fine. The important ingredients are the nuts, chilies and salt. If you are allergic to cashew nuts like I am, substitute with peanuts.

SERVES 4 ◦ PREP TIME: 10 MINUTES ◦ COOKING TIME: 5 MINUTES

2 cups (500 ml) unscented oil
3 cups (350 g) cashew nuts
3–5 kaffir lime leaves, shredded
Coriander leaves (cilantro), handful of the leaves and cut stems
3–5 bird's eye chilies, sliced, any color
1 teaspoon sea salt
Juice of 1 lime, to taste

In a hot wok, heat the oil until smoking, then add the cashews and kaffir lime leaves and fry until the lime leaves are crispy and the nuts golden.

Remove and drain on paper towels. Then toss the nuts in a bowl with the coriander leaves, chilies and salt. Taste for seasoning.

Squeeze the lime juice over the nuts right before serving and taste for seasoning again.

Serve immediately with a nice cold beer, maybe one that has been in the freezer until it achieves a jelly-like consistency (it's called *beer woon*, or "beer jelly").

The Portuguese Influences in Thai Food

In the 15th and 16th century, nuns in Portugal crafted sweets called conventual sweets, made from egg yolks that were left over after using egg whites to starch their habits. These egg yolk-based conventual sweets would be sold to sweet-toothed customers by the nuns for extra pocket money. It is these sweets, created by Christian nuns, that would become the traditional Thai desserts known as *tong yip* (golden balls), *tong yod* (golden drops) and *foy tong* (golden threads).

The desserts were brought to Siam courtesy of Maria Guyomar de Pinha, a Bengali-Portuguese-Japanese woman who was eventually enslaved in the kitchens of the usurper king Phetracha following the Siamese Revolution of 1688. But Portuguese influence was not limited to this one cook. The Portuguese were inveterate travelers credited with bringing a plethora of ingredients to Thailand, like papayas, chilies, pineapple, corn and cashew nuts—all things now deemed intrinsic to Thai cuisine.

But the Portuguese influence on Thailand is not shown merely through cooking. The Bangkok neighborhood known as Kudichin started out as a parcel of land granted by then-King Taksin to the Portuguese, who were known for being loyal to the throne. Made up largely of Portuguese and other ethnic groups who moved to Bangkok after Ayutthaya's fall, the Kudichin neighborhood centers around Santa Cruz Church and remains home to the initial settlers' descendants even today.

"That is what is now Kudichin: it's a mixture of the Chinese that were there, the Portuguese descendants, and the Muslims that were living there," said Francisco Vaz Patto, who served as Portuguese ambassador to Thailand. "So in this area you can find the influence of the three cuisines and the three communities living together. That is an amazing example of coexistence between communities in Thailand."

Minced Chicken Kanom Jeen

You will not find this dish anywhere outside of the Kudichin neighborhood in Bangkok. It's a mild yellow curry with ground chicken smothering fermented rice noodles. It is mild and tasty, delicious with the addition of some fried Chinese sausage slices on top. I've included paste ingredients (to be made in a food processor), but store-bought mild yellow curry paste is also fine.

SERVES 4 ● PREP TIME 35 MINUTES ● COOKING TIME: 10 MINUTES

2 tablespoons unscented oil
1 lb (approx 500 g) ground chicken
1–2 cups (250–500 ml) coconut milk
   (enough to cover the chicken)
1 tablespoon shaved palm sugar or
   white sugar
1–2 tablespoons tamarind juice
   (page 29)
Fish sauce, to taste
8 oz (200 g) *kanom jeen* (Mon-style
   fermented rice noodles), or rice
   vermicelli (soak the vermicelli in
   a pot of boiling water with lid on,
   submerge the vermicelli in water,
   turn heat off and wait for 8
   minutes), drained and portioned
   into individual serving bowls
Coriander leaves (cilantro), to garnish
Deep-fried Chinese sausage slices,
   to garnish (optional)

Curry Paste

4 small Thai shallots, or 1–2 small
   regular shallots
4 heads Thai garlic, or 1 head large
   regular garlic bulb
5–10 bird's eye chilies, depending
   on spice tolerance
3–4 inch (7.5-8 cm) piece ginger,
   peeled and chopped
3 tablespoons lemongrass, tender
   inner part of bottom third only,
   finely sliced and smashed in a
   mortar and pestle
1 tablespoon salt, or to taste
2 tablespoons ground turmeric
3 tablespoons curry powder
2 teaspoons ground coriander

Make the **Curry Paste** by peeling the shallots and garlic and roasting them with the chilies in a pan or the oven until slightly charred and soft. Then buzz together in a food processor with the ginger and lemongrass until everything is well incorporated. Add the salt, turmeric, curry powder and coriander and buzz again. If the food processor becomes stuck feel free to add a couple of tablespoons of water to loosen the paste so it can be thoroughly blended.

Heat the oil in a wok or large pan over medium heat, add the Curry Paste and cook until aromatic. Add the ground chicken, coat well with the paste and cook until the chicken is no longer pink. Add the coconut milk, sugar and tamarind juice and stir to incorporate. Let it bubble over low heat until everything is well incorporated and the flavor infuses the milk, about 10–15 minutes. Taste for seasoning and add the fish sauce and more salt if necessary. It should not be very spicy.

Ladle over the rice noodles and garnish with coriander leaves and Chinese sausage slices (if using).

Hearty Beef Tongue Stew

This stew might seem like a strange addition to a Thai cookbook, but I promise you this is something Thai people actually eat, at old-fashioned cookshops or old chain restaurants like S&P (the Thai equivalent of a "diner"). Basically, it's the Thai equivalent of meatloaf—stodgy and old-fashioned, never cool, but strangely satisfying. The original dish is basically Portuguese with Thai ingredients, which might not be so appealing to cooks who already live in the West, so Lauren zhushed the recipe up by adding Asian aromatics to a classic European stew.

SERVES 6 ● PREP TIME: 30 MINUTES ● COOKING TIME: 3.5–4 HOURS

1½ lbs (approx 700 g) ox tongue (already peeled by butcher). Beef shank or any good stew meat may be substituted

1 tablespoon salt

2 tablespoons + 1 tablespoon vegetable oil (olive preferable)

2 onions, peeled and sliced

3 cloves garlic, minced

1 cup (250 ml) red wine

3 cups (750 ml) beef stock

3 cinnamon sticks

5 cardamom pods

4 bay leaves

2 star anise

5 whole cloves

1 teaspoon black peppercorns, smashed

1½ tablespoons peeled and grated fresh ginger

1 stalk lemongrass, tender inner part of bottom third only, smashed

1 tablespoon shaved palm sugar

2 tablespoons soy sauce or Maggi Seasoning

2 large carrots, peeled and cut into thirds

1 cup (200 g) peeled canned tomatoes with juice

3 potatoes, peeled and cut in half

1 cup (150 g) peas (frozen is fine), optional

2 tablespoons flour or 2 teaspoons cornstarch

Salt and pepper, to taste

Fresh coriander leaves (cilantro) and sliced bird's eye chilies, to garnish

Soak the meat in cool water with a tablespoon of salt for 20 minutes, then rinse and pat dry.

Slice the meat into thin slices going across the grain of the meat to create rectangular shapes roughly ½" thick x ½" wide x 1½" (1.25 cm x 1.25 cm x 3.75 cm) long.

Heat 2 tablespoons oil in a Dutch oven over medium high heat. Add the onions and cook for 15 minutes, stirring frequently, until caramelized. Add the garlic and brown lightly. Remove the onions and garlic and set aside.

Add 1 tablespoon of oil to the pot. Working in small batches, sear the meat until well browned on all sides, removing each batch and placing to the side when finished. Do not over stir. Let the meat sear. Make sure not to overcrowd the pot with meat as well or it will release too much water and begin to poach rather than sear.

When finished cooking the meat, remove the Dutch oven from the heat and pour off any fat, but retain the browned bits. Place the pot back on the stove and pour in the wine, scraping the bottom of the pot to loosen the browned bits.

Cook on medium heat until the liquids reduce by half, then turn the heat to low and add the stock. Return the reserved meat, onions and garlic to the pot. Add the cinnamon sticks, cardamom pods, bay leaves, star anise, cloves, black peppercorns, grated ginger, bruised lemongrass, palm sugar and soy sauce or Maggi Seasoning. Bring the contents to a gentle simmer.

Heat the oven to 275°F (135°C). Transfer the pot, with its contents, to the oven. Add the carrots, tomatoes and potatoes. Cook for another 3 hours until the potatoes are soft and the meat is very tender. Add more stock or water to the pot as needed to keep the stew at a soup-like consistency. Add the peas right before serving making sure they are well drained and are warmed thoroughly.

Remove the pot from the oven. Remove if desired any unwanted aromatics (lemongrass, cinnamon, bay leaves, star anise, etc) for eating ease.

Using a ladle, remove half cup of liquid from the simmering pot and place on medium heat in a small saucepan. Using a whisk, stir in the flour or cornstarch. Cook for 5 minutes stirring frequently, then stir in more liquid from the stew to dilute the flour mixture and ensure there are no lumps. Pour the mixture back into the stew and mix. The stew should be thicker, but not gummy.

Add salt and pepper to taste. Serve with hot steamed rice, topped with coriander leaves and bird's eye chilies.

CHAPTER 3
Northern Thai Cooking

Where China, Laos and Myanmar Meet

Once known as the kingdom of "Lanna" ("A million rice fields"), Northern Thailand was the last of the parcels of land to be incorporated into Siam, the country that would become Thailand. Because of that, its culinary identity remains specific and distinct from the rest of the nation, where coconut milk, chilies and shrimp paste rule. Here, in the "cooler" climes that dominate the North's mountains and forests, it's all about the bitter greens and vegetables that make up the local flora, and one more thing: pig, pig, and more pig.

"Chickens are for laying eggs, and cows are put to work," said Northern Thai food expert Chatree Duangnet, who is also my dad. "Pork ends up being the food that you eat when you want to have a great meal. It is fatty and rich. It is also the food of the northern aristocracy."

Although bordered on two sides by Myanmar and Laos, Northern Thailand is most influenced by its northern neighbor China, where many of its inhabitants originated from the 18th century. Such is the influence of Chinese settlers on the local cuisine that the base flavor of many Northern Thai dishes is Chinese: fermented soybean discs known as *tua nao*, or "rotten beans." Considered the Northern equivalent to the shrimp paste, *pla rah* (fermented Thai anchovies) or *nam bu du* (Southern Thai fish sauce) used in other parts of Thailand, *tua nao* is usually sold in dried round chips that are broken up and added to curry pastes, broths and chili dips to form some of the North's most iconic dishes, including Nam Ngiew Pork and Tomato Sauce Noodles (page 105).

That's not to say that 200 years of being colonized by neighboring Burma haven't left their mark. A staple starch in the region, *kanom jeen* (fermented rice noodles), came courtesy of the Mon, who once occupied parts of what are now Thailand and Myanmar hundreds of years ago. *Khao ganjin*, known commonly among visitors as "purple rice," is a popular breakfast food filched from the Shan tribe in Burma. It is made of rice cooked in pig blood and garnished with deep-fried garlic oil, dried chilies, fresh lime and sliced shallots. Another famous dish, *khao soy* (see Khao Soy Curried Egg Noodles with Chicken, page 59), is said to be modeled after noodles found commonly in Myanmar today.

Of course, there are also some Laotian influences in the mix, although they have been very Sinocized. Northerners boast their own version of *larb* (page 98), a minced meat dish commonly found in Isaan.

Saa Pak Northern Mixed Salad

My Aunt Priew makes this out of 13 ingredients found in the forest during the rainy season. This is probably not a realistic thing to truly replicate when living abroad, since even in Bangkok ingredients like these are hard to find. I'm including it anyway because it is one of my very favorite dishes in the world, and can stand up to savvy substitutions relatively unscathed.

SERVES 4 ▪ PREP TIME 30 MINUTES ▪ COOKING TIME: 10 MINUTES

10 round Thai eggplants (or anything crunchy and willing to stand up to a strong dressing, like deseeded cucumbers, zucchini, kohlrabi, or summer squash, or a mix with some asparagus and/or even artichoke bottoms)

2 teaspoons salt dissolved in 2 cups (500 ml) water

6 finger-length chilies (*prik chee fah*, if available)

3 Thai shallots (or 1 regular shallot)

1 head Thai garlic (or about 4–6 cloves regular garlic)

1 teaspoon shrimp paste (*kapi*)

2 tablespoons Thai anchovies (*pla rah*), canned anchovies will do, (optional)

1 stalk lemongrass, tender inner part of bottom third only, thinly sliced

1 tablespoon *nam puu*, or Northern Thai chili paste (It's unfortunately very hard to locate in stores, even in Thailand). If you don't have any, add a little more shrimp paste to taste

Deep-fried Pork Rinds (page 131), for garnish

If you are using Thai eggplants, slice each in half and scoop out the seeds with a spoon. Then slice what's left thinly (a Japanese mandoline helps), along with any other vegetables you decide to use.

Everything in the salad should be thinly sliced. Soak the vegetables in salt water. With your hands, "massage" the vegetables well in the water. Drain and rinse and set aside.

Roast the chilies, shallots and garlic in an oven or pan for 3–5 minutes until the skins are blackened. Allow to cool and then peel the chilies, shallots and garlic.

Wrap the shrimp paste and Thai anchovies (if using) in aluminum foil and roast until aromatic, about 5 minutes. Little by little, pound the roasted ingredients together in a mortar and pestle until a paste is formed. Decant into a large bowl.

Add the eggplant (or other vegetables), along with the sliced lemongrass and the *nam puu*, if using. Mix well. Serve immediately, garnished with the pork rinds.

A Day in the Life of a Chiang Rai Market

Chiang Rai is often considered the middle-aged aunt to Chiang Mai's younger, prettier ingenue. The first capital of King Mengrai's dynasty, it was abandoned in favor of Chiang Mai ("new town") in 1296. But Chiang Rai's under-the-radar status has given it some silver linings. Its wet markets—unlike the colossally crowded Warorot Market in Chiang Mai—are filled to the brim with culinary offerings unlikely to be found anywhere in its southern sister city, and its walkways are only half as crowded. This makes for a pleasant way to spend the morning when you don't have to fight with other tourists for a slice of fried pork cutlet.

Even mid-morning, Talad Baan Mai ("Wooden House Market") remains serene but busy, although popular vendors like the *nam prik nam pak* (vegetable juice chili dip) man have already sold out. Beyond the toys and horned beetles sold as playthings for curious children lies a cavernous room in which vendors spread out five rows across, side to side. Along the perimeter are the live animal vendors; vats of freshwater eels in inch-deep water and tiny frogs that await their fates next to flapping fresh fish gasping in shallow plastic tubs.

Vegetable vendors display wares that go beyond the usual lime leaves and water olives, one literally selling pond scum, dried into a bright green powder meant to go into a chili dip. Another sells fragrant *noi pokadaek* (a garlic-like  bulb that tastes like room deodorizer), meant to refresh the palate and freshen the breath; yet another is a purveyor of the Northern Thai equivalent of shrimp paste, *nam puu*, the black juice strained from pulverized rice field crabs. Ant eggs to be blanched or boiled in stews and soups are sold during the rainy season; silkworm grubs are offered up for frying and eating with beer. Perhaps most eye-opening of all are the bee larvae, still encased in honeycomb. No one would accuse the Northern Thais of not being resourceful when it comes to food.

Gang Pak Plang Soup with Pork Sausage

This is more of a soup and less of a curry. Scratch that: it's not a curry at all. It's light and refreshing, even with the fermented pork sausage.

SERVES 4 • PREP TIME: 1 DAY (BEST IF LEFT TO CURE OVERNIGHT IN THE BRINING LIQUID)
COOKING TIME: 1 HOUR

3 cups (750 ml) water

¼ cup (60 g) Chili Paste

1 lb (400 g) fermented pork sausage (*naem*), cut into bite-sized pieces (if you cannot source *naem*, try German teewurst)

2 cups (200 g) flowers and soft stems of the *plang* plant (basella alba), washed. Cauliflower florets, okra or asparagus may be substituted

2 Northern Thai green chilies (*prik num*) or 4 finger-length chilies (*prik chee fah*, if available), roasted, peeled and sliced

4 red plum tomatoes, quartered, or 8 cherry tomatoes, halved

Fish sauce, to taste

2 tablespoons lime juice

Chili Paste

1 big dried chili

½ teaspoon salt

5 Thai shallots, peeled (1 if using regular shallots)

5 cloves Thai garlic (if using regular garlic use 1–2 cloves), peeled

1 teaspoon shrimp paste (*kapi*)

Make the **Chili Paste** by pounding the dried chili with the salt until a paste is formed. Add the shallots, garlic and shrimp paste and pound to incorporate. Reserve ¼ cup for use in this recipe and store the rest in an air-tight jar in the fridge for future use.

In a pot, boil the water over medium heat. When it starts boiling, add the Chili Paste to infuse the water with the flavor. Once the Chili Paste has dissolved, add the fermented pork sausage pieces, followed with the *plang* plant pieces and submerge them completely.

Add the chilies and tomato. Bring to a boil again and cook at a healthy rolling boil until the vegetables are tender. This should take around 40–45 minutes. Turn off the heat.

Taste for seasoning and if still bland, add some fish sauce to taste. To improve the flavor, I'd recommend transferring this curry to a plastic container and keeping it in the refrigerator overnight.

On the next day, reheat the fermented sausage and curry in a pot. Once warmed through, scoop out the sausage and vegetables. Set aside. Continue heating the curry until it is reduced to 2 cups.

Return the sausage and vegetables to the pot. Taste for seasoning and add fish sauce and lime juice if necessary. The flavor should be tart, salty and a little bit spicy. Serve with Sticky Rice, grilled meat and a chili dip as part of a Northern Thai meal.

How to Cook Sticky Rice

When making Sticky Rice, Thais use a straw hood called a *huad*, but we tried with a sieve and a pot and it worked! First get uncooked short-grain sticky rice and soak the desired quantity (½ cup per serving) overnight. If you don't have the time, soak it in boiling water for 20–30 minutes.

Then drain and pour (another) potful of boiling water over the rice to cover. Stir the grains to prevent them from getting sticky, for 5 minutes, or until they become slightly translucent. Drain through a fine mesh sieve and place the sieve (with the rice grains) across a stock pot filled with an inch of water. Cover the pot with a lid. Steam for 20–30 minutes (this method takes longer than the regular method with a woven bamboo steamer). Set a damp dish towel over the lid if there is a gap between the cover and pot because of the sieve.

Halfway through, toss the grains or give them a stir.

When done, spread over a wet flat surface like a tray to cool, making sure to turn handfuls of the rice with a rice paddle occasionally to get rid of steam so that the rice will not be soggy.

Best to consume as soon as possible. If not, put it in a bowl and cover with plastic wrap and place in the fridge until ready to reheat.

Here are **rice cooker directions** if you are short on time, however, please know results will not be quite as good. Place the rice in a rice cooker and cover with tepid water. Let sit for 40 minutes and up to 4 hours. Sticky rice has a hard outer shell that needs to soften to achieve the best texture once cooked.

After sitting, stir the rice and water quickly before turning the rice cooker on. When your rice cooker switches off, let the rice sit at least 5 minutes longer.

Once ready to serve, toss the rice with a paddle to release the steam and fluff up.

Pik Gai Tod Baab Fried Chicken Wings

A lot of recipes call for marinating the wings, but the best ones I know are by my housekeeper, Somporn. She simply dips the wings in seasoned flour briefly and deep-fries them. This is her recipe.

SERVES 4 ◦ **PREP TIME: 30–35 MINUTES** ◦ **COOKING TIME: 10 MINUTES**

2 lbs (1 kg) chicken wings
1 cup (150 g) all-purpose flour, seasoned with salt and pepper
2 cups (500 ml) vegetable oil
Salt and pepper, to taste
Jaew Chili Sauce (page 34), to serve
Sticky Rice (page 90), to serve
Sliced red chilies and coriander leaves (cilantro) for garnish, optional

Heat 2–3 inches (5–7.5 cm) inches of oil in a pan or wok to fry temperature: 350°F (175°C).

Dredge the wings in the flour, then fry the wings in batches until golden brown, about 10 minutes per batch.

Drain on paper towels and transfer to a plate. Season with salt and pepper to taste.

Garnish with sliced red chilies and coriander leaves, if using.

Serve immediately with Jaew Chili Sauce and Sticky Rice.

Nam Prik Ong Minced Pork

This is known by some people as "Thai Bolognese" because of its resemblance to the Italian meat ragu. It is not meant to be spicy and is most often eaten with pork rinds, boiled cabbage wedges and sticky rice.

SERVES 4 ● PREP TIME: 25 MINUTES ● COOKING TIME: 10 MINUTES

3 dried chilies, soaked and cut into 1-inch (2.5-cm) pieces
2 small shallots, peeled and minced
4 cloves garlic, peeled
2 coriander (cilantro) root, chopped
1 tablespoon chopped galangal
1 tablespoon shrimp paste (*kapi*), wrapped in aluminum foil and roasted in oven for 3–5 minutes until aromatic, or 1 tablespoon fermented soybean disc (*tua nao*), pounded to a paste
½ lb (250 g) ground pork
4 cherry tomatoes, chopped
2 tablespoons unscented oil, for frying
½ cup (125 ml) water

2–3 tablespoons fish sauce
Handful of fresh coriander leaves (cilantro), minced
Deep-fried Pork Rinds (page 131), boiled cabbage wedges, Sticky Rice (page 90), to serve

In a mortar and pestle, pound the chilies, shallots, garlic, coriander root, galangal and shrimp paste or fermented soybean disc (*tua nao*).

Add the ground pork and mix to combine. Add the tomatoes. Bruise with the pestle, mixing into the pork and seasonings.

Heat the oil in a wok over medium-high heat and add the pork mixture. Fry until everything is cooked, about 5–6 minutes. Add the water and mix. Bring to a boil before reducing the heat. Simmer until the dip is almost dry. Add the fish sauce to taste.

Once the tomatoes have given up the ghost and are shells of their former selves, the dip is done.

Garnish with coriander leaves and serve immediately with the accompaniments.

Nam Prik Num Roasted Green Chili Dip

This is usually eaten with pork rinds, sticky rice, hard-boiled eggs and boiled veggies like pumpkin wedges and green beans. My Thai food mentor, Chef McDang, says the young Northern Thai chilies in Thailand are a lot hotter during the dry "cool" season (December–February). This is his recipe.

SERVES 4 • PREP TIME: 15–20 MINS • COOKING TIME: 5 MINUTES

15 young Northern Thai green
    chilies (*prik num*) roasted on
    a baking tray in the oven and
    peeled after cooling
5 small shallots, roasted and peeled
10 cloves garlic, roasted and peeled
2 tablespoons mashed anchovies or
    other salted fish meat
1–2 tablespoons fish sauce
1 tablespoon lime juice
1 teaspoon shaved palm sugar

Deseed the chilies if you wished to reduce the spice level.

In a mortar and pestle, pound together the chilies, shallots and garlic.

Add the anchovies, fish sauce, lime juice and palm sugar. Mix well and taste. Flavors should be salty and spicy.

Gang Gradang Cold Pork Jelly

This recipe presents quite a challenge and different cultures have this "meat jelly" in their cuisines. Northern Thailand is no different. This adds a different texture to a typical family spread. It's eaten family style with everything else, alongside stews, soups, salads, chili dips, fried pork and sticky rice. To be honest: I had every intention of including the "easier" Chiang Mai version. My father (a Chiang Rai native) said that this would be a terrible disservice to you, the cook, so here I am with the more complicated Chiang Rai version, which includes a spice paste.

SERVES 6 ◆ PREP TIME: 3 HOURS PLUS JELLY OVERNIGHT SET TIME ◆ COOKING TIME: 2½ HOURS

1–2 pig trotters (about 1 lb/450 g)
6 cups (1.5 l) water
2 teaspoons salt
½ cup (65 g) Spice Paste
Handful of coriander leaves (cilantro), for garnish
Handful of sliced green onions (scallions), for garnish

Spice Paste

6 dried red chilies, deseeded and then soaked in water until soft
1 teaspoon salt
2 tablespoons minced galangal
3 stalks lemongrass, tender inner part of bottom third only, sliced
3 coriander (cilantro) root
30 cloves Thai garlic (or about 15 cloves regular garlic)
5 Thai shallots, sliced (or around 2 regular shallots)
2 teaspoons shrimp paste (*kapi*)

Roast the pig trotters in the oven at 350°F (180°C) until the skin is cooked and the flesh is firm, approximately 30 minutes.

While the trotters are roasting, make the **Spice Paste**. In a mortar and pestle, bash the dried chilies with the salt until well incorporated. Add the galangal, lemongrass and coriander root and mash together until a paste is formed.

Then add the remaining ingredients slowly and in the order listed until everything is well mixed together. Reserve ½ cup for this recipe and store the rest in an airtight jar in the fridge for future use.

Remove the trotters from the oven and scrape off any hair by either torching with a blow torch or soaking in water.

In a large pot add 6 cups water, the trotters, salt and ½ cup of Spice Paste. Cook slowly over low heat for 2½ hours, until the trotters is extremely soft. Remove the trotters and let cool. Once cool, remove the bones and slice the trotters into bite-sized pieces.

Pour the contents of the pot into a square casserole dish and add the meat from the trotters. Allow to cool and keep in the refrigerator (preferably overnight) until it sets and forms a jelly. Cut into squares and serve, garnished with fresh coriander leaves and sliced green onions.

Sai Oua Chiang Mai Sausage

This was one of the first Thai recipes I learnt—so desperate was I to have this gorgeous herbal sausage in my freezer. I first learned to make this with the help of my friends Chris (who had a meat grinder attachment) and Jarrett, who used to let us make coils of the sausage in the kitchen of his much-lamented restaurant, Soul Food Mahanakorn.

SERVES 10–12 • TOTAL PREP TIME: 2½ HOURS • COOKING TIME: 45 MINUTES–1 HOUR

20 feet (7 meters) sausage casing or 20 individual sausage casings
2 lbs (approx 1 kg) ground pork
2 lbs (approx 1 kg) ground pork fat
5 shallots, minced
5 cloves garlic, minced
8–10 kaffir lime leaves, finely sliced
1 tablespoon finely sliced or grated lemongrass, tender inner part of bottom third only
1 cup (50 g) coriander leaves (cilantro)
¼ cup (32 g) peeled and minced fresh turmeric (careful, it will stain your hands yellow)
½ cup (30 g) chopped sawtooth coriander (optional)
¼ cup (32 g) dried chilies, soaked and minced (or more if prefer spicier)

4 tablespoons pre-mix Southern Thai orange curry paste, mixed with 4 tablespoons pre-mix yellow curry paste (store-bought is fine)
1 teaspoon salt, to taste
3–4 tablespoons fish sauce, to taste

Rinse the sausage casings and then soak in warm water for an hour.

Mix all the ingredients, except the sausage casings, together. Taste the sausage mix by frying a little of it in a pan with a little vegetable oil; adjust seasoning if necessary.

Stuff the sausage casings either by hand or with a sausage stuffing machine, twisting the ends to seal. It should make about 20 sausages.

To cook the sausages, prick each link with a fork and bake in the oven at 400°F (200°C). Bake until the sausages turn a burnished brown, the color of mahogany, approx 45 minutes to 1 hour.

Sausages may also be grilled. Serve with Sticky Rice and a chili dip, ideally Nam Prik Num Roasted Green Chili Dip (page 93) and some fresh vegetables.

Northern Thai Communal Larb Culture

Out of all the dishes made in Thailand, perhaps none is as symbolic of deep community ties as *laap*, also known as *larb*, or *larp*, or even *laab*. Cooking is often a solo affair, its product the struggle of a cook alone in the kitchen with the pot, fire and whatever happens to be in the larder. The traditional process of making *larb*, however

(and in the interests of this book, we'll go with the most common spelling of the dish, if not the most correct), is an act that involves many, from the butcher of the animal to the cook who perfects the seasoning. As a result, *larb* often serves as a punctuation mark to celebrations, the glue around which people in the village can rally in the pursuit of getting fed.

"*Larb* is one of those dishes in Asian popular cuisine where the food is more than just a meal, but an integral part of one's culture," wrote Dr. Hanuman Aspler of thaifoodmaster.com. "A feast believed to facilitate good health and bring good luck, an enjoyable time spent among friends, neighbors and relatives."

Known primarily as a spicy-tart salad of ground chicken or pork from Isaan, *larb* is more of a description of a cooking technique than of the dish itself, denoting a ground protein cooked in shallow liquid. And although *larb* is most commonly served abroad in its Northeastern Thai incarnation, it comes in many different guises throughout the North and Northeast, mirroring the different influences that have wended their way through the regions over the years.

In Isaan, *larb* is a quick and easy dish that ("all together now") packs maximum punch with minimal effort. The combination of flavors—sour, salty and herbaceous—makes it delicious when paired with Sticky Rice and fresh vegetables, or even when eaten alone. In Northern Thailand, on the other hand, *larb* betrays all the influences of

traders from the Silk Road, a deep mahogany mish-mash of cinnamon, star anise and dried chilies tinged with hints of blood, best enjoyed with the bitter green leaves of the surrounding forest.

Although Thailand's history of pairing food with alcohol is sparse, *larb* is one of the few dishes created specifically to pair with beer or spirits. The ingredients in *larb*, when mixed with *ya dong*, the potent medicinal alcohol brewed specifically to address certain ailments, are even meant to improve men's health (or are marketed that way). Because of this, it is also traditionally made by men, for men, of all economic strata, from all parts of society.

"Boozing is still primarily a male vice, especially on the lower rungs of society," noted Andy Ricker of Pok Pok. "Big city, high society social patterns follow Western ones pretty closely these days, especially in Bangkok, so the split between genders is not that noticeable. But go hang

out at the gate of a construction site at night and you'll likely see the workers drinking *lao khao* (Thai moonshine) just like their country cousins."

To address this particular niche in Thai cookery—the Thai version of a men's club-slash-steakhouse—a whole sub-strata of restaurants exists to serve *larb* paired with alcohol. Called *larb luu lao*, they offer the eponymous ground meat salad; *saa*, featuring sliced meat; *lu*, a dish of meat, blood, spices, herbs and, if it's beef or buffalo, bile; and *lupia*, a dish in which the blood is replaced by gastric juices. Many of these dishes are served raw, and the accompanying alcoholic drinks are supposed to help kill any germs.

Surprisingly, the addition of "bitter bile" ends up sweetening the meat, adventurous gourmets say. "If there's a bitter option, I always go for it," said Mark Wiens of eatingthaifood.com. "Perhaps it's an acquired taste, but somehow bile is both bitter and sweet, and balanced. It's just amazing how Thais have managed to find a way to use every single part of an animal and ingredient, to balance and complement ingredients in a dish."

But if you don't have a hankering for a mouthful of bloody raw meat, it's OK; these restaurants have you covered there, too. Instead of *larb dib*, or raw *larb*, you can order Minced Pork or Beef Larb, in which the meat is cooked in a wok without oil (our recipe on page 98).

Minced Pork or Beef Larb

This is traditionally made with pig blood to give it that deep mahogany color but of course you don't need to include the pig blood.

SERVE 4–6 ● PREP TIME 45 MINUTES ● COOKING TIME: 10 MINUTES

1 teaspoon coriander seeds
1 teaspoon fennel seeds
2 bay leaves
2 star anise
½ stick cinnamon
4 cardamom pods
1 teaspoon *makwaen* (a type of Sichuan peppercorn)
10–14 chopped dried chilies
10 cloves garlic
3 red shallots
1 teaspoon shrimp paste (*kapi*)
Ten ½ inch (12.5 mm) slices galangal, peeled
2 stalks lemongrass, tender inner part of bottom third only
1 lb (450 g) ground pork or beef
1–2 tablespoons pig blood (if using pork, optional)
1–2 tablespoons vegetable oil
¼ lb (100 g) ground pork liver (if using pork) or calf liver (if using beef)

1–2 tablespoons cleaned and boiled pig intestine (if using pork) or beef tripe (if using beef), optional, cut into little pieces
1–2 tablespoons fish sauce, or to taste
Salt, to taste
Chopped mint and coriander leaves (cilantro), whole sprigs of mint

Garnishes

Sticky Rice (page 90), to serve
Lettuce leaves, cabbage leaves, sliced cucumbers and lime wedges (not too much lime for this *larb* though—unlike Isaan *larb*, northern Thai *larb* is more salty and spicy)

Dry roast the spices (coriander seeds, fennel seeds, bay leaves, star anise, cinnamon, cardamom pods, and *makwaen* peppercorns) in a wok. Once roasted, place in a mortar and pound, add the dried chilies.

Roast the garlic and shallots, place in the mortar with the shrimp paste, galangal and lemongrass and pound with a pestle into a paste. Set aside.

Further mince the pork or beef on a chopping block with a butcher's knife. If using pig blood, sprinkle 1–2 tablespoons of the pig blood onto the pork as you are mincing it, adding to the deep red color of the meat. This will help to develop both the flavor and the color of the pork.

Heat a wok until smoking hot and add 1–2 tablespoons vegetable oil. Swirl around, add the spice paste and meat. Mix everything together, and cook stirring occasionally until the meat is well browned, approx 10–15 minutes. Add 1 tablespoon of water once the meat is browned to deglaze the pan.

Add the liver and intestines or tripe to the wok. Add more oil if needed. Cook for 2–3 minutes. Add the fish sauce to taste. If too dry (the juices should collect at the bottom of the wok like the dressing for a very juicy salad), add a little water. If you do not want to add more fish sauce, add the salt instead. The flavor should be salty, spicy and intense.

When the taste is to your satisfaction, add fresh chopped mint and coriander leaves (cilantro) and mix.

Garnish and serve at room temperature with Sticky Rice and fresh lettuce, cabbage and cucumbers.

Minced Fish Larb with Herbs

I'll admit it: I don't do the bile or blood salads. When I find myself in a macho *larb* restaurant, I always end up ordering the fish *larb*, and it's always incredibly delicious. This one is inspired by the *larb* I had at Raan Larb Pa Tan in Chiang Mai.

SERVES 4 ● PREP TIME 20 MINUTES ● COOKING TIME: 5 MINUTES

1–2 cups (250–500 ml) water
1 lb (approx 400 g) firm, white-fleshed fish that is hopefully also sustainable, like barramundi or hake
3 tablespoons fish sauce
2 tablespoons lime juice
2 teaspoons chili powder (*prik pon*), or to taste
½ cup (50 g) sliced shallots (or ¼ cup (25 g) if using regular shallots)
¼ cup (25 g) chopped green onions (scallions)
¼ cup (10 g) chopped fresh coriander leaves (cilantro)

2 tablespoons ground roasted rice kernels (page 34)
Fresh mint leaves, for garnish (optional)
Sticky Rice (page 90), to serve

Boil the water in a large saucepan and add the fish meat. Poach quickly, around 1–2 minutes so that the fish is cooked through but not dry. Remove from the heat. Drain and place the fish on a serving plate, it will naturally break into large bite-sized pieces, if not gently break them apart.

Combine the fish sauce, lime juice, and chili powder in a bowl. Taste and adjust seasoning if need to. Pour this sauce over the fish.

Add the shallots, green onions and coriander leaves. Mix together well. Add the roasted rice kernels and mix well again.

Serve on a plate, garnished with fresh mint leaves if you have them. Serve with Sticky Rice.

Chiang Mai's Midnight Fried Chicken Restaurant

Ask anyone who has been lucky enough to grow up in Chiang Mai in recent decades, and chances are they frequented this late-night restaurant on a regular basis. "Everybody went there as a kid," they would invariably say. "Don't even try to get there before midnight."

Alongside spots like Khao Soy Lamduan Faham, Samerjai, and Huen Phen, the restaurant known in Thai as "Khao Nung Gai Tod Tien Kuen" (quite literally, "Sticky rice fried chicken midnight") stands among the pantheon of truly famous eating spots in the city. Yet in spite of its city-wide fame, the English-language name of this inconceivably famous restaurant is in dispute. While it seems most well-known as "Midnight Fried Chicken," it is also known as "Midnight Sticky Rice" and even "Midnight Fried Pork."

In short, this restaurant has a handful of famous dishes for which it could be named, all served at midnight.

Because Chiang Mai's nightspots had a reputation for closing early, Midnight Fried Chicken opened after they closed their doors, gaining a reputation for feeding hungry barflies who were in no hurry to go home. Eventually they became so popular they opened a second branch with different operating hours, but the original famously kept its doors open throughout the night, until early-bird vendors started setting up shop at 5 a.m. the next morning.

Set in an unassuming dark area that brings to mind something out of Wong Kar-wai's *Chungking Express*, Midnight Fried Chicken can also be spotted by following the long queue forming outside the eatery, patiently waiting

for the door to be opened at midnight. Then like clockwork, diners will be seated at one of the tables, most of which lined the road. By the light of a few dim light bulbs they scrutinize a small-type menu in Thai, putting checkmarks next to all the items they wanted.

Besides fried chicken and sticky rice, the other popular dishes were the deep-fried pork ribs, deep-fried three-layer pork, and if you were the adventurous sort, deep-fried (sensing a theme here) pork intestines, known as chitterlings in the United States.

Everything was meant to be eaten with hot sticky rice and a garlicky paste called *nam prik tha dang* ("red eye" chili dip) as well as the Northern Thai standby *nam prik num* (roasted green chili dip). That, and the garnish of pickled greens and blanched cabbage, would be the extent of all the vegetables on the menu.

The advent of COVID has changed a lot for everyone in Chiang Mai, Midnight Fried Chicken among them. This eatery, known for being up all night, now opens its doors at 7 p.m. in the evening, although the smiling server greeting us tonight says that they will start opening up at 6 p.m.

There is no more queue in front of the shop, with impatient and hungry locals awaiting their chance to snag a table. Half of the tables have disappeared, and the ones that have remained are mostly empty.

But what hasn't changed is the menu: delicious, deep-fried meats of all persuasions, accompanied by hot sticky rice and delicious chili dips.

The eatery now does a good trade in take-out, and is even on local food delivery app Food Panda. Like every nimble business nowadays, Midnight Fried Chicken has adapted to the changing times, feeding a new generation of kids.

Nam Prik Tha Dang "Red Eye" Chili Dip

The best version of this chili dip—literally translated as "red eye chili dip"—bar none, is at Midnight Fried Chicken in Chiang Mai. In fact, my mother and I both stock up on this whenever we go there, hauling kilos of the stuff back on the plane home. Luckily, Thai customs officials are very understanding about that kind of thing when it comes to food.

SERVES 4 ● **PREP TIME 15–20 MINUTES** ● **COOKING TIME: 5 MINUTES**

7 big dried chilies

4–7 small Thai shallots, peeled (if using regular shallots reduce to 2–4 small)

2 heads Thai garlic, peeled (if using regular garlic, use 1 small head)

2 tablespoons Thai anchovies (*pla rah*), regular anchovies if Thai anchovies is not available

2 teaspoons salt

3 tablespoons dried grilled fish, flesh only, already pounded (Thais use roasted snakehead fish or catfish flesh)

Accompaniments

Fresh cabbage, Thai eggplants, blanched oyster mushrooms

Deep-fried Pork Rinds (page 131)

Over a low heat, roast the dried chilies in a pan until aromatic and crispy, being careful all the while not to burn them. Set aside.

Roast the shallots and garlic until very aromatic and slightly charred. Set aside to cool.

Wrap the anchovies in *nam wah* banana leaves or aluminum foil and roast until fragrant.

In a mortar and pestle, pound the dried chilies with the salt until well ground. Add the shallots and garlic and pound well to incorporate.

Add the anchovies and dried fish and pound until everything is well mixed together. Decant into a bowl and serve with the suggested accompaniments.

Moo Tod Fried Pork Cutlets

This is quite literally "fried pork" and yes, it's basically schnitzel without the bread crumbs, pounded to within an inch of its life and deep-fried. There is nothing better than this for sticky rice and an assortment of chili dips with vegetables. When we are in Chiang Rai, my former nanny Pong always buys this at the market as part of a big meaty spread for breakfast (!)

SERVES 4 ● PREP TIME 25 MINUTES ● COOKING TIME: 10 MINUTES

2 lbs (1 kg) pork chops, without
   bone (raw pork scallopini cutlets)
3 large eggs
1 tablespoon fish sauce
1 tablespoon ground black pepper
1 cup (250 ml) unscented oil like
   canola
½ cup (75 g) all-purpose flour (or
   more if needed)
1 head garlic, coarsely cut (skins
   can still be on)
Sticky Rice (page 90), to serve

Place the chops between two pieces of waxed paper on a cutting board and pound until thin with a meat tenderizer, pestle or pan. Get it as thin as possible.

In a large bowl, beat the eggs.

Season with the fish sauce and black pepper.

Heat the oil in a wok until hot. Dredge the cutlets in the flour, then into the egg and deep-fry the cutlets (about 2–3 minutes per side. Best to err on the side of caution without actually burning

them). Set on a paper towel-lined plate to drain.

Fry the garlic in the oil until crispy. Scatter over the pork when done.

Serve on a platter with plenty of Sticky Rice and chili dips with vegetables.

The Story of Thai "Spaghetti"

It is a widely accepted fact that good Northern Thai food is hard to find in Bangkok. This is not a bunch of sour grapes from people in the North like me who all of a sudden find themselves stranded in the hurly-burly world of the capital. It's because, according to my dad, Northern Thai people are cheapskates. And because they are cheapskates, they don't go out to eat very much, and since they don't go out to eat very much, there is very little incentive for restaurants in the Big City to serve good Northern Thai food—particularly if they are not Northern Thais themselves.

For this reason, I have had a touch-and-go relationship with the Northern Thai restaurants in Bangkok, which is a shame, because that is where I live now. Everywhere I go, I order Kanom Jeen Nam Ngiew, a rice noodle dish slathered in a pork "gravy." But everywhere I get it, I find it wanting. I think it's an unfair task I am setting up for these places. After all, it's hard to beat your favorite food memories. And the dish my dad calls "Thai spaghetti" is my biggest food memory of all.

Truth is, I want to find The One that will bring me back home. Home to New Castle, Pennsylvania, where I wanted to dine on cavatelli ("ca-vads") like everyone else in my predominantly Italian-American town. Home, where I would see my dad in his pajamas stuffing his own *sai oua* (recipe on page 95) on the floor of our kitchen and feel unaccountably embarrassed. Home, where my dad would have to refer to *nam ngiew* as "Thai spaghetti" to get us to eat what he cooked after a 14-hour work day.

And it does resemble bolognese, after a fashion. It is typically made with the fermented Mon-style rice noodles found all over the South called *kanom jeen*, but you can also find it served with rice noodles, just like they appear to do in Laos (where, to make things more interesting, they call it *khao soy*). The sauce is made of ground pork with tomatoes, chilies, shallots, garlic and fermented soybeans and the noodles are topped with fresh bean sprouts and coriander (cilantro) leaves.

In the North, they add well-stewed pork ribs, cubes of congealed pig blood and the requisite *dok ngiew* flowers, witchy-looking blossoms that resemble broomsticks and lend a chewy texture and floral taste to the brew. If one is lucky, the ribs are cooked until the bones have nearly disintegrated into the sauce, the blossoms are thick and plentiful, and the dish comes to you with a generous dusting of deep-fried garlic. Just add a squeeze of lime and go to town.

Nam Ngiew Pork and Tomato Sauce Noodles

This is a great dish for a party or large family gathering.

SERVES 10 ⬥ PREP TIME: 35 MINUTES ⬥ COOKING TIME: 20 MINUTES

2 lbs (1 kg) pork spare ribs, cut into 1 inch (2.5 cm) pieces
2–3 tablespoons cooking oil
2 lbs (1 kg) ground pork
2 lbs (1 kg) whole cherry tomatoes
Optional additions: Dried *ngiew* blossoms, cooked pig blood, black taucheo or fermented brown bean sauce (*tao jiew*).
Fish sauce, to taste
Lime juice, to taste
1 lb (450 g) *kanom jeen* (Mon-style fermented rice noodles, store-bought, and kept moist under a damp dishcloth), or 1 package spaghetti, cooked according to package instructions
For garnish: deep-fried chopped garlic, chopped fresh shallots, lime wedges, pickled greens, and deep-fried dried chilies (optional)

Nam Prik

30 pieces dried red chilies
30 dried bird's eye chilies
4 medium shallots
25 cloves garlic
½ cup (100 g) shrimp paste (*kapi*)
3 stalks lemongrass, tender inner part of bottom third only
1 tablespoon salt
1 cup (120 g) grilled dried fermented soybean disc (*tua nao*), pounded (if not possible to obtain, add a little more shrimp paste instead)

Blend the ingredients for the **Nam Prik** in a food processor. Set aside.

Fill a medium pot one third full with water and bring to a boil. Add the spare ribs and cook for about a minute until slightly soft but not cooked through. Remove from the water, reserving the cooking liquid.

In a large pot or wok, fry the Nam Prik mixture in hot oil until it "smells fragrant" and tickles the inside of your nose. Add the ground pork and spare ribs. Stir until the meat is cooked through. Add about 3 cups of the reserved cooking liquid to the wok. Then add the tomatoes and cook until the tomatoes go soft but still are holding their shape, around 5 minutes. Add the optional additions, if using.

Add fish sauce and lime juice to taste. Serve immediately on *kanom jeen* (fermented rice noodles) or spaghetti, garnished with garlic, shallots, lime wedges, pickled greens and dried chilies (if using).

CHAPTER 4
Isaan Cuisine from the Northeast

Influences from Laos and Vietnam

American Chef Dan Barber once said that the greatest cuisines of the world are born out of poverty and necessity. The food of the Northeast region is Thailand's version of this type of cuisine. Unlike the rest of the country, which is verdant and fertile, parts of Isaan are dusty and dry, and the food—strong, spicy, quick to make, sugar-less—reflects that. Like the perfect 3-minute pop song, it is direct and makes a big impact.

I like to say that Isaan cuisine is "gregarious" and "straightforward," the perfect dinner party guest. What I mean by that is that Isaan's spicy, tart, and salty flavors are almost always bona fide crowd pleasers that get the job done with minimum angst or fuss. Need something to fill the stomach after a hard day's work? Set a pot of water to boil with some chicken on the bone and handfuls of herbs and chilies and fish sauce and you've got yourself a meal with sticky rice. Feel a little peckish in the morning? Light a fire and grill a nice fatty tranche of pork collar, flavored with some fish sauce and coriander (cilantro) root.

Little surprise, then, that what I like to call Isaan food's "holy trinity" (the trifecta of grilled chicken, green papaya salad and sticky rice) marks some of the most popular foods eaten by the Thais themselves. It's also widely prevalent on the streets, where a vast majority of Thais buy at least one thing a day. It is very, very difficult not to get your hands on some

grilled chicken or minced *larb* salad during a 15-minute walk up any street in Bangkok.

The popularity of Isaan food is even starting to take off beyond Thailand's borders. Indeed, the first Michelin star ever awarded to a Thai-owned restaurant went to an Isaan place: Somtum Der in New York City. However, what goes unmentioned are the specific influences of other countries on Isaan cuisine, especially from neighboring Laos, original home of *som tum* (grated papaya salad) and *larb* (ground meat salad). Immigrants from next-door Vietnam also had a hand in the cuisine, leading to breakfast staples like *guay jab yuan* (Vietnamese hand-rolled noodles in a clear broth) and *moo yaw* (steamed pork paté). What Isaan did—and what Thais often invariably end up doing—was put its own spin on the cuisine, making something unique in the process. The result is a food, born out of poverty, that may end up taking over the whole world.

Por Pia Tod Spring Rolls

The filling for this recipe is Isaan-style chicken *larb*, which, I was surprised to learn, is not typically seasoned with lime juice. That addition is a Bangkok thing. Instead, Isaan *larb* is meant to be spicy and salty. In any case, you have the option of adding lime juice at the end, (just like us Bangkokians). This recipe also works with ground pork.

SERVES 6 ◦ **MAKES APPROX 20 SMALL SPRING ROLLS** ◦ **PREP TIME 15 MINUTES FOR LARB, 40 MINUTES FOR SPRING ROLLS** ◦ **COOKING TIME: 5 MINUTES**

1 package spring roll wrappers (frozen is fine). If using a whole package of 50 wrappers consider doubling the Chicken Larb recipe
1 teaspoon cornstarch dissolved in 1 tablespoon warm water
2 cups (500 ml) vegetable oil
Jaew Chili Sauce (page 34)
Thai Sweet Chili Sauce (page 46)

Chicken Larb

3 tablespoons water
½ lb (250 g) ground chicken
2–3 small shallots, thinly sliced (you can use red onion instead)
3 fresh coriander leaves (cilantro) and stems, chopped
3 sawtooth coriander (if you have them), chopped
3–4 kaffir lime leaves, thinly sliced
1–2 tablespoons roasted rice kernels (page 34), ground to a powder
1 teaspoon salt
1 tablespoon fish sauce
1–2 tablespoons chili powder (*prik pon*)
Juice of 1 lime (optional)

To make the **Chicken Larb**, heat a saucepan until a drop of water sizzles on it, then add the water. Add the chicken immediately. After the juices come out of the meat, the bits of chicken will stop sticking to the pan. Cook through until the pink is all gone.

Transfer the chicken and it's juices to a mixing bowl and add the shallots, coriander leaves, sawtooth coriander, kaffir lime leaves and roasted rice powder. Mix everything well together well.

Add the salt and fish sauce. Taste for seasoning. Add the chili powder. Taste and adjust as needed.

If you wish, add the lime juice, mix well and taste. You can now eat your Chicken Larb if you don't want to make your spring rolls. Just garnish with mint leaves and enjoy with Sticky Rice (page 90), young cabbage leaves, fresh cucumber and long beans!

Otherwise, set the Chicken Larb aside as filling for the spring rolls.

Thaw the spring roll wrappers (if frozen) and keep under a damp kitchen towel. Peel the top one off to start. With the smooth side down, place the wrapper in a diamond shape and place a spoonful of the Larb at the bottom of the diamond. Roll up halfway, fold both sides in towards the center, then continue rolling up to the top. Seal with the cornstarch mix. Repeat until the Larb is used up.

Heat the oil in a wok until very hot, then put in a layer of the rolls, making sure the oil is double the depth of the rolls. Fry them in batches, turning occasionally until golden brown, around 1 minute. Drain each batch on paper towels when done. Serve with Jaew Chili Sauce or Thai Sweet Chili Sauce.

Gang Om Lemongrass and Dill Chicken Soup

Grang om is something the workers put to the pot after work when they are hungry and need a quick meal. You eat it with sticky rice. (Note: there is also a Northern Thai version of *gang om* which includes a chili paste base of dried chilies, galangal, lemongrass, coriander root, coriander seeds, turmeric, garlic, shallots and shrimp paste.)

SERVES 4 ● PREP TIME 25–35 MINUTES ● COOKING TIME: 10 MINUTES

Paste

5 shallots
3 finger-length chilies
1 stalk lemongrass, tender inner
    part of bottom third only

Soup

1 tablespoon unscented oil
1 chicken breast, chopped into
    2-inch (5-cm) size pieces
4 chicken wings
1 chicken carcass, broken up (about
    2 lbs/900 g)
1 stalk lemongrass, tender inner
    part of bottom third only, bruised
1–2 chicken bouillon cubes
3 oz (85 g) carrots, optional
3 oz (85 g) baby corn, optional
½ cup (50 g) sliced mushrooms,
    optional (or any other vegetables)
Fresh dill, 1–2 big handfuls
Fish sauce or *pla rah* (fermented
    Thai anchovies), to taste
1 tablespoon roasted rice kernels,
    page 34 (optional)

Pound the **Paste** ingredients in a mortar until a paste is formed.

To make the **Soup**, place the Paste and 1 tablespoon unscented oil in a medium pot and fry until aromatic. Add the chicken breast and wings and mix to coat thoroughly with the Paste.

Add the chicken bones, lemongrass and bouillon cubes to flavor. Add enough water to just cover the contents in the pot.

Once the Soup is boiling, add the veggies in order from longest to cook to shortest, if using. Add the dill. Add the fish sauce to taste. (If adding *pla rah*, must make sure the soup is boiling well, or the soup will smell). Boil for around 10 minutes or until all the chicken pieces and veg-gies (if using) are cooked through.

Remove the chicken bones from the pot. Before serving, add the roasted rice kernels (if using) to give the soup a roasted smell. You can eat this immediately or heat it up later. If eating later, do not add the rice kernels until ready to serve.

Makuea Mashed Eggplant Salad

Our housekeeper Somporn makes a mean mashed salad out of the Thai eggplants left over from the chili dip from the day before. If you don't have Thai eggplants, purple eggplants will do.

SERVES 4 ● PREP TIME 20–25 MINUTES ● COOKING TIME: 10 MINUTES

4–5 small shallots with skins on, roasted in a pan or oven
6–8 Thai eggplants, boiled until well softened through (If not available substitute 2 small-sized purple eggplants, roast drizzled with unscented oil until soft)
2 tablespoons chili powder (*prik pon*)
2 teaspoons kaffir lime leaves, julienned
3 tablespoons roasted rice kernels (page 34), ground
1–2 tablespoons *pla rah* (Thai anchovies) juice (or fish sauce, if you're in a pinch)
Juice of 1 lime, to taste (optional)
1 handful each of chopped mint, coriander leaves (cilantro) and sawtooth coriander

Remove the shallot flesh from the skins. With your mortar and pestle, mash the shallots until they are like a jam.

Remove the eggplants from their outer skin. Add the flesh to the mortar and mash until they are of the desired consistency. Mix in the chili powder, kaffir lime leaves, and ground roasted rice kernels.

Flavor with *pla rah* or fish sauce. Add the lime juice to taste. Add the chopped herbs and mix in well. Serve at room temperature with Sticky Rice (page 90), crunchy raw vegetables like cucumber, and grilled meat.

Pla Rah and its Importance in Isaan Cooking

Few people would argue that *kapi* **(shrimp paste)** is the key to Central Thai cuisine, but many of those people still studiously avoid the fermented Thai anchovies known as *pla rah*. Meant to provide an extra oomph to a grated *som tum* salad or the verve to a quick *gang om* soup of herbs and chicken, this flavoring is so revered among Northeastern Thais that some would argue that any dish without the signature funk of *pla rah* is not truly Isaan at all.

Originally known among locals as *pla daek*, or "chopped fish," *pla rah* is usually made by cutting up a large fresh fish (or a handful of small fish), removing the organs, scales, fins and the head, and mixing the pieces with salt and rice bran or roasted rice kernels before placing them into an earthenware jar and storing it in a dark, cool place for up to a year. The juice that results from this fermentation process is salty and fishy, full of a deep, dark flavor that is also packed with umami. Unfortunately, the smell is something that takes some getting used to.

Thais in ancient times did not harbor such scruples. Indeed, *pla daek* was so prized that it was used as a form of currency. The name was changed to *pla rah* by Central Thais because the word *daek* is an impolite term for "to eat." All the same, Central Thais even today are not overly fond of the seasoning, pointedly omitting it in their own version of *som tum thai* (the inclusion of the word "Thai" in the name suggesting that *pla rah* may, in fact, not be considered "Thai.")

I remember working with a Dutch man who mentioned that one of the personal hazing rituals for expats that he encountered was to advise them to order *som tum* without mentioning the type of *som tum* they wanted was the Thai kind. "If I didn't like them, I made sure they got the other kind," he said, meaning the more authentic Isaan version with *pla rah*. Although his expat associates may not have appreciated it, I personally have grown to prefer the Isaan version of *som tum*, which I see as rawer, more immediate, and far more flavorful than its gentrified counterpart.

"Isaan salads (*tum*) should have *pla rah* to make it Isaan," said Bangkok-based tour guide Chin Chongtong (foodtoursbangkok.com), who originally hails from the area around Ubon Ratchathani. "But if some don't like it they can use fish sauce, not *pla rah*. I'm not sure if you can say it's Isaan food or not, but it's not exactly Central Thai either."

As for other dishes in the Isaan culinary lexicon, *pla rah* is something that you can either take or leave. On the "optional" list is the Isaan dipping sauce *jaew*, the spicy condiment used to flavor a variety of grilled meats. Dishes that don't make use of the fermented fish at all include the Isaan-style *hor mok*, a steamed "casserole" wrapped in banana leaves and made with banana flowers, *tom saap*, a wildly spicy soup most frequently made with pork ribs, and Vietnamese-inspired dishes such as Moo Yaw (Pork Paté) and Kai Kata (Egg in a Pan).

But for food lovers who adore the smell and taste of *pla rah*, nothing compares to the real thing. Thai cooks who ferment their own fish must take the jar out every 10 days or so to mix the fish pieces with a wooden paddle especially made for that purpose. Those without the patience to undergo this task for 12 months must "improve" upon the store-bought variety by boiling it with pineapple, shrimp paste and tomato for about two hours, Chin advises.

Besides *som tum*, other ways of using up that hard-won fermented fish is to chop up the flesh and juice with a battery of julienned herbs like kaffir lime leaves, lemongrass, shallots, and chilies to make *pla rah sub* (literally "minced *pla rah*"), which is eaten with plain white rice and fresh vegetables like Thai eggplants.

Foolproof Som Tum Pla Rah

It's hard to believe, but I really think I am lucky enough to have one of the best cooks of Isaan food in Bangkok at my own home. Her name is Somporn, and she has been my mother-in-law's trusted helper for almost 40 years. During lunches with my in-laws, Somporn is basically a one-woman restaurant, whipping up *som tum* dishes in keeping with everyone's personal preferences (extra sour and not spicy for my mother-in-law, Thai-style with no chilies for my son, extra chilies for my husband, and with *pla rah* for me). This is her recipe for Som Tum Pla Rah.

SERVES 2–4 DEPENDING ON THE AMOUNT OF SALAD INGREDIENTS USED • PREP TIME 20–25 MINUTES COOKING TIME: 5 MINUTES

Dressing

Juice of 1 lime
3 tablespoons tamarind pulp, thinned out with a few teaspoons of hot water
2 tablespoons *pla rah* (Thai anchovies, optional), or you can puree anchovies and strain through a sieve to obtain the liquid, fish sauce may also be substituted
2 cloves garlic
½–1 tablespoon shaved palm sugar
Fresh bird's eye chilies (2 is standard, 4 is my current level, 5 is my husband's, and 20(!) is the most I've ever seen)

Salad

Anything crunchy and julienne-able, e.g. ⅓ of a small green papaya, half of a large carrot, 3–4 plum tomatoes, handful of cut-up long beans, corn kernels

Garnishes

1 handful roasted peanuts (optional)
1 handful fresh coriander leaves (cilantro) and/or mint leaves, washed (optional)
Fresh white cabbage leaves
5–10 long beans, cut into 2-inch (5-cm) pieces
1 washed and unpeeled cucumber (or 2 small cucumbers), sliced

Put all the **Dressing** ingredients in a mortar. Taste to adjust seasoning. Add the **Salad** ingredients and pound hard with the pestle to bruise the strands of the papaya (to release some of the sap into the Dressing).

If your mortar is not large enough, the Salad ingredients and Dressing may be mixed together in a separate bowl. Upend onto your serving dish and eat as soon as you can.

Garnish with roasted peanuts or fresh herbs like coriander and mint leaves and accompanied by a platter of fresh vegetables to cut the spiciness, if you like.

Som Tum Salad and Its Makeover in the Capital

It is almost impossible to live anywhere in Bangkok that is not within walking distance of a *som tum* vendor. While street food lovers frequently rhapsodize over the best bowl of noodles or grilled hunk of meat, it's this grated, pounded salad made of fruits and vegetables that most often finds itself on Thai tables.

Although the grated green papaya *som tum* is the variety that is most popular in (and outside) Thailand, local vendors display a wide range of fruits and vegetables on their carts with which to make this salad, from cucumbers and long green beans to tart gooseberries and green bananas. Even snails and *kanom jeen* (fermented rice noodles) have been known to join in the fun. The truth is, just about anything could make a good base for a grated spicy salad. It's the dressing that usually stays constant.

That dressing, and the pounding needed to turn a salad into a *som tum*, require a *krok* (mortar and pestle). The best

som tum cooks jealously guard their mortars and pestles for generations, much like a chef would guard his omelet pan, or a Japanese *oden* vendor guard his broth. I've been told the very best mortars and pestles are made of tamarind wood, and that ceramic or stone ones are too hard on the delicate strands of vegetable or fruit, turning your salad into a gloppy mess. If you can, invest in a good wooden one that you can pass on from generation to generation, pounding good salads all the while.

Bangkok is most known for *som tum* Thai, the type of *som tum* most commonly eaten in the capital and abroad. Ironically, the very Bangkokians who decry the prevalence of "fusion" Thai cuisine probably still enjoy "*som tum* Thai"—a salad that Northeastern Thai people might see as a fusion of its own, created after the first Isaan vendors settled in Bangkok and set up shops around the Victory Monument area. Made up mostly of green papaya and a dressing of lime juice, fish sauce, and a healthy dose of sugar (be it palm or granulated), the salad also features a light dusting of roasted peanuts and dried shrimp. Notably absent? *Pla rah* or the fermented anchovies deemed integral to Isaan cuisine.

Central Thai-style Fruit Som Tum

This is one instance where not using the mortar and pestle for the fruit will probably help you. The only thing that should be bruised here, besides the dressing, is the long bean.

SERVES 4 ● PREP TIME: 15 MINUTES ● COOKING TIME: 5 MINUTES

2–4 small bird's eye chilies (or to taste depending on desired spice tolerance)
2 tablespoons shaved palm sugar
1–3 small cloves garlic, peeled
3 tablespoons fish sauce
2 tablespoons lime juice
1 tablespoon dried shrimp, ground to a powder in the spice grinder
3 tablespoons roasted peanuts, coarsely chopped

Salad

1 cup (100 g) long beans, cut into inch-long (2.5 cm) lengths and bruised in a mortar and pestle
1 cup (150 g) cherry tomatoes, halved
1 cup (150 g) seedless grapes, halved
1 cup (200 g) apple or pineapple, cubed
1 cup (175 g) pomelo or orange, cut into bite-sized pieces

Place the chilies in a mortar and pestle and grind, then add the palm sugar and garlic cloves and pulverize.

Next add the wet ingredients: fish sauce and lime juice and mix together. Set this dressing aside.

In a bowl add the **Salad** ingredients and the dried shrimp powder. Spoon over the dressing and mix together. Decant onto a plate. Garnish with the roasted peanuts.

How the Vietnamese Came to Isaan

Many visitors to Thailand don't realize that the "Land of Smiles" is really more of a patchwork quilt of ethnicities and nationalities than it may seem at first glance. Home to a sizeable chunk of Japanese expatriates, the South Asian diaspora and a thriving Muslim community, Thailand also claims a longstanding Vietnamese presence in its Northeastern region. That community, established in the late 1800s, is part of the reason why the food of Isaan is so vibrant and dynamic.

Because of its central location, the Isaan region has borne a number of foreign rulers in its time. First was the ancient Khmer empire; following the Khmers came the Laotian "Lan Xang" (a million elephants) dynasty. Only then did the Siamese take over, and during the Vietnamese War, the American military established a firm presence there in a *de facto* colonization.

Many think that the Vietnamese came to Thailand during the Vietnamese War, but in fact the community is much more deep-rooted than that. The first community of Vietnamese settlers came when the French colonized Vietnam in the 1880s, setting up homes in relatively bigger towns like Ubon Ratchathani, Sakhon Nakhon and Nakhon Phanom. They called themselves the "Viet Kieu" (overseas Vietnamese).

The second wave came after World War II ended and France re-established its hold over Vietnam. The third followed soon after, when Northern Vietnam fell to the Communists in 1952. The "Viet Kieu" broadened the scope of places they settled in, to Udon Thani, Nong Khai and, eventually, Mukdahan. Today, these towns are still known as the main network for Vietnamese settlers in Thailand.

While the Chinese eventually were able to assimilate into the Thai population—especially after Thailand's ultra-nationalist period of the 1930s and '40s—the Vietnamese community seemed to face more obstacles from the locals at first, particularly politically. The "Viet Kieu" were seen as actively advocating for revolution from their outposts in nearby Isaan, as well as being pro-Communist, a definite no-no in a region where the U.S. military built bases.

There also seemed to be a culture clash between the industrious Vietnamese and their more laid-back neighbors which, naturally, included Thailand. According to Donald Wilson on the website CPA Media (cpamedia.com), there is a familiar saying that "Lao + Viet = cat + dog." This could very well extend to the Cambodians and Thais alongside the Laotians.

Whatever friction may have taken place before in Thailand's history, it has certainly dissipated now, with the presence of the Vietnamese extending like a backbone all through the Isaan region. Wilson writes that Nong Khai now resembles parts of French Indochina, while smaller hamlets such as Tha Bo—or any other town boasting a Christian church—harbor a sizable number of Vietnamese families. At Tha Phanom, markets are held every week, attracting Laotian and Vietnamese vendors including purveyors of the famous Vietnamese sandwich *banh mi*, referred to in Thai as *khao jii*. Meanwhile, the town of Sri Chiang Mai is known as the "spring roll capital of Thailand" for its central role in manufacturing rice paper wrappers for the rest of the country. Business is, presumably, booming.

Moo Yaw Pork Paté

This recipe is not actually Thai—it's Vietnamese. Thais have since taken the Vietnamese *cha lua* and put their own spins to it, like dressing it in chilies, fish sauce and lime juice and making it into a salad.

SERVES 6 ◆ PREP TIME 1 HOUR 15 MINUTES PLUS OVERNIGHT TO FREEZE SAUSAGE MEAT ◆ COOKING TIME 45 MINUTES

2 lbs (1 kg) pork loin
2 tablespoons potato starch
2 tablespoons unscented oil
2 tablespoons fish sauce
2½ teaspoons baking powder
1 teaspoon sugar
1 teaspoon white pepper
4 tablespoons water

Cut the pork into small pieces and puree in a food processor. Add the rest of the ingredients and puree again until well incorporated.

Put the puree in an airtight container and freeze overnight. The next day, remove from the freezer and allow to thaw. Grind the meat one more time in a food processor in batches. Divide the meat into 6 equal portions. Wrap each portion in aluminum foil (or banana leaves if you have them). Shape into logs, each no more than 1 inch (2.5 cm) in diameter. Tie with kitchen twine but leave lots of extra space at the ends as the sausages will puff up to double its size when cooked.

Fill a large pot, big enough to hold all the logs, with water. Bring to a boil, add the pork logs and cook for about 40 minutes.

Pull out a log and checked if it is cooked by cutting off one of the ends. The meat should turn beige, not pink. Remove the cooked sausages, cool and refrigerate.

Now you can use what you've made and prepare it in a distinctly Thai way: in a delicious, spicy and tart salad.

Moo Yaw Salad

4 oz (100 g) glass vermicelli (*woon sen*)
½ cup (100 g) Moo Yaw Pork Paté (recipe on left), cut into bite-sized pieces
1 cup (100 g) chopped cabbage
1 tomato, chopped
½ onion, chopped
3 tablespoons chopped Thai celery, (or just the leaves of the celery stalks)
Green onions (scallions), chopped, for garnish
Roasted peanuts, for garnish

Dressing
2 tablespoons fish sauce
1 tablespoon lime juice
1 teaspoon sugar
2–4 bird's eye chilies, crushed or sliced, depending on your heat tolerance

Soak the glass vermicelli in boiling water for about 3 minutes or until completely soft. Drain well.

Make the **Dressing** by mixing the fish sauce, lime juice and sugar together. Taste and adjust seasoning if necessary. Add the chilies. Set aside.

Combine the Moo Yaw, glass vermicelli, cabbage, tomato, onion and Thai celery in a large bowl. Drizzle with the Dressing and mix well to combine. The Dressing should be abundant, but not soak the salad completely.

Garnish with the green onions and peanuts. Serve immediately.

The Royal Gift of Tilapia (from Japan)

One of the most famous and oldest sayings in Siam is an inscription dating back to the Sukhothai Era, more than 600 years ago, basically reading "there is fish in the water, and rice in the fields." Whether the inscription is truly genuine or not, the premise is the same: Thailand is a land of abundance and fertility, never lacking in food for its people.

Thailand did face a protein shortage in its rural provinces during the middle of the past century, enough to prompt the Japanese then-Prince Akihito to send over 50 Japanese tilapia that he hoped would flourish in Thai waters. Although 40 died on the way to Thailand, the remaining 10 were kept at Chitralada Palace by King Bhumibol Adulyadej. These became the forebears to the most popular Tilapia breed farmed in Thailand today—the *pla nin* (derived from its English-language name, the Nile River fish). From then on, said King Bhumibol, even the poorest of Thais would be able to have access to fish, a nutritious and versatile protein.

In the Isaan region, Thais took the tilapia fish and gifted the rest of the country with *pla pow*, or salt-encrusted grilled fish. The tilapia is gutted and stuffed with lemongrass and kaffir lime leaves, then coated with a mix of flour and salt and grilled over a low but steady flame. When the fish is cooked (about 20 minutes on each side), the salty skin is cut open to reveal glistening, tender flesh that can be enjoyed with any number of dipping sauces. Today, these grilling fish are a common sight on the sidewalks of every town in Thailand.

Although *pla pow* is lovely to eat as part of a big Isaan meal, or even on its own with steamed rice, I prefer it as part of one of my favorite Thai street side dishes, *mieng pla*. There are several types of *mieng pla*, one with fried Thai mackerel, but I prefer the other one with the grilled salt-encrusted tilapia. The fish is accompanied by lettuce leaves, herbs and maybe some thin rice noodles, rolled up Korean barbecue-style and adorned with your choice of dipping sauce, some peanuts, and maybe some slivered ginger. It's one of the best meals I know, and two kings helped make that happen.

Obviously, it's great with seabass or grouper too. Choose a firm, white-fleshed fish that won't fight with the flavors of the all-important dipping sauces (up to three!). Because I hate being hot, I include an option for baking the fish, Mediterranean-style, in the oven under a mound of sea salt. It works! And it's easy.

Mieng Pla Pow Baked Fish

Normally, these salt-encrusted fish can be found streetside, grilling over hot coals. Because I am not one to slave away over the grill, I have tweaked this recipe to using the oven. However, if you do want to do the hot coals thing, Mark Wiens has a recipe on his website, eatingthaifood.com, for *pla pao*, the dish that we are seeking to emulate (eatingthaifood.com/thai-grilled-fish-recipe-pla-pao/).

SERVES 6 ■ PREP TIME: 1 HOUR ■ COOKING TIME 40 MINUTES

1 whole (approx 6 lbs/2½ kgs) seabass, grouper or tilapia, gutted, scales still attached
3–6 kaffir lime leaves
3 stalks lemongrass, tender inner part of bottom third only, bruised
1 pandanus leaf, or the green part of a leek, wrapped around the aromatics with kitchen twine
2–4 lbs (1–2 kgs) coarse salt
Dipping Sauces, see page 120

Garnishes

Lettuce leaves, preferably green oak or butter, coriander leaves, basil, mint, sawtooth coriander (if you have it) bird's eye chilis, rice vermicelli, ginger, slivered, roasted peanuts, chopped fresh shallots.

Preheat oven to 390°F (200°C).

Stuff the aromatics bundle into the fish, which has been patted dry.

Place the fish in a baking pan with a shallow layer of salt already on it and encase the rest of the fish in salt completely like you have murdered it and are trying to hide the evidence.

Bake for 30 minutes, then allow to rest for 10 minutes.

Make the Dipping Sauces by following the recipes on page 120.

Fillet the fish into skinless boneless pieces and arrange on a platter with the garnishes and Dipping Sauces.

Garnishes are meant to be eaten with the fish flesh. The pieces of fish are wrapped in the leaves, bulked up with rice noodles, garnished with pieces of fresh ginger, fresh herbs and roasted peanuts, and seasoned with Dipping Sauce.

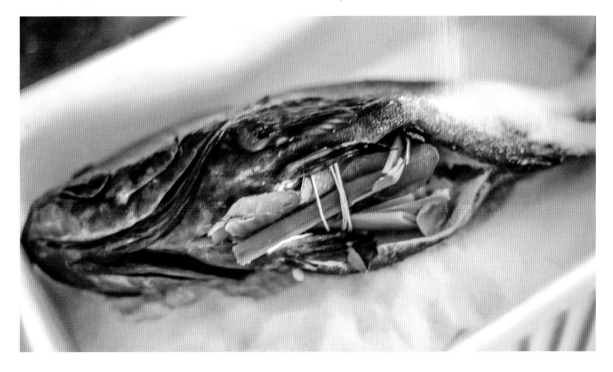

Mieng Pla Pow Dipping Sauces

Nam Prik Tua Thad

Tua thad is a type of Thai peanut brittle made with roasted peanuts, sesame and palm sugar. So imagine my surprise when my friend Tawn made a *nam prik* out of it! It was delicious and surprisingly, my favorite combo. If you don't have this Thai snack, regular peanut brittle should do, but watch the sugar level.

4 bird's eye or finger-length chilies
    (*prik chee fah*)
2 coriander (cilantro) root, cleaned
7 cloves garlic, or to taste
6 pieces *tua thad*, or peanut brittle
Juice of 2 limes
3 tablespoons fish sauce
1 teaspoon honey or golden syrup

In a mortar and pestle, pound the chilies, coriander root and garlic together into a paste. Scrape out of the mortar and set aside.

Pound the peanut brittle until

it is pulverized, then add the chili paste. Mix well. Season with the lime juice and fish sauce. Taste. It should be a balance between salty, acidic, spicy and sweet.

Add the honey or golden syrup if it is not sweet enough. Surprisingly, the sweetness will amplify all the other flavors.

Nam Prik Macaam

This dipping sauce is made from tamarind paste and is the more traditional of the sauces you will find to accompany this dish. It has the same base as *tua thad*.

4 bird's eye or finger-length chilies
    (*prik chee fah*)
2 coriander (cilantro) root, cleaned
7 small cloves garlic, or to taste
2 tablespoons tamarind paste
Juice of 1 lime
3 tablespoons fish sauce
3 tablespoons shaved palm sugar
Water (as needed)

In a mortar and pestle, pound the chilies, coriander root and garlic together into a paste. Add the tamarind paste, lime juice, fish sauce and palm sugar. Taste to adjust seasoning. If the sauce is too thick, add a little warm water to thin.

Seafood Dipping Sauce (recipe on page 33)

This is the other traditional dipping sauce used in tandem with the tamarind paste one. Thais can't get enough of their sauces!

Kai Kata Egg in a Pan

This recipe was inspired by the Vietnamese vets who came over into Thailand on their breaks and requested American-style breakfasts from local cooks. The cooks' efforts, which utilized local ingredients, have become popular all on their own in the Northeast, where this is a popular street food breakfast.

SERVES 2 ⊕ PREP TIME 10-15 MINUTES ⊕ COOKING TIME: 5–10 MINUTES

2 well-buttered ramekins
2 soft rolls (see recipe on page 152 or use rolls of your choice)
Butter, for the rolls
1 link Chinese sausage, sliced
6 slices Moo Yaw Pork Paté (page 117), or baloney
2 4 eggs depending, on size of ramekins
Salt and pepper, to taste
Maggi Seasoning and/or fish sauce, to taste
Sriracha Chili Sauce (page 31), to taste
Green onions (scallions), sliced, to garnish and/or coriander leaves (cilantro)

Preheat oven to 325°F (180°C).

Place the rolls, sliced open and buttered, into a casserole and toast in the oven until warm and the butter melted.

In a pan, warm the Chinese sausage and Moo Yaw Pork Paté or baloney until hot.

Crack 1–2 eggs into each ramekin and cook in the oven for 5–10 minutes, until the whites are cooked and the yolk done to your liking.

Garnish the eggs with 4 slices of Chinese sausage and 2 cut-up Moo Yaw Pork Paté slices. Season with salt and pepper.

Fill the toasted rolls with leftover slices of Moo Yaw Pork Paté and Chinese sausage.

To serve, season the eggs with Maggi Seasoning/fish sauce/ Sriracha Chili Sauce to your taste. Serve with the toasted rolls on the side.

CHAPTER 5
Southern-style Favorites

Southern Thailand: "Soldier's Rations"

Nakhon Sri Thammarat native Chef "Ice" of Sorn likes to say that the food that he serves at his two-Michelin-starred restaurant is the simple cuisine of his Southern Thai hometown. It's what he calls "soldier's rations."

But as simple as those rations may have started out to be, his food is now acclaimed enough to have won Sorn global accolades and a months-long waiting list. This is the paradox of Southern Thai cuisine: simple ingredients and a straightforward premise, but razor-sharp execution.

The main principles of Southern Thai cuisine are easy enough to get. Ingredients, including just-plucked-from-the-ocean seafood, must be of the utmost quality. Recipes are not muddied with a plethora of ingredients like in Central Thai cuisine; but what ingredients do make the cut have to deliver the maximum when it comes to flavor. And what you get is often ear-ringingly, eye-wateringly spicy, enough so that plenty of that white, fluffy rice is needed to lessen the sting.

It's easy to get full from a Southern Thai meal, provided you have the rice (and maybe a fluffy deep-fried omelet or two) to see you through all the chili dips and fiery stews. Maybe this is why it's considered such a humble cuisine: if pressed, cooks can whip up a meal with a handful of baht.

Luckily for Southern Thailand, the region is awash with an abundance of choice ingredients. The ground and trees yield plenty of greenery to accompany the many chili dips of the South, greens like the leaves of the mango tree and the cashew tree, fresh stink beans (*petai*) still in their pods, and a multitude of crunchy baby eggplants. Young coconuts yield fresh white flesh, perfect for bulking up a soup or curry; when in a pinch, papayas or pineapples will also do. Jackfruit are deep-fried into tasty fritters eaten on the street; bean sprouts and cucumbers are pickled to accompany rich coconutty curries piled on top of fermented rice noodles, a typical Southern Thai breakfast.

Of course, don't forget the local seafood. Meaty tranches of deep-sea pomfret and seabass adorn turmeric-rich soups speckled with dried chilies. Crabs and their eggs are also curried, or simply boiled and served with a spicy-tart dipping sauce. Phuket lobster is steamed with myriad Thai herbs. Squid and shrimp are grilled or deep-fried or, in some cases, piled on top of fluffy omelets to help soak up all that fire. Even fish innards are pickled or fermented, flavoring soups and stews, made into curries, or made into a dressing for salads. Anything from the sea goes, when it comes to Southern Thai cooking.

Yum Woon Sen Glass Vermicelli Salad

This recipe comes courtesy of my mother-in-law's sister, who serves this at every large family gathering to great acclaim. Thanks to the coconut milk and deep-fried shallots, it's a creamier and sweeter take on the usual glass noodle salad.

SERVE: 5–6 ◦ PREP TIME: 40 MINUTES ◦ COOKING TIME: 10 MINUTES

8 oz (approx 250 g) glass vermicelli (*woon sen*)
1 lb (approx ½ kg) shrimp, cleaned and minced or finely chopped
Unscented cooking oil, for frying
1 lb (½ kg) Thai shallots (approx 14 shallots). If using regular shallots, use ½ lb (225 g) or 3–4 large shallots, peeled and sliced
2 cups (500 ml) coconut milk
⅓ cup (65 g) shaved palm sugar
2½ tablespoons fish sauce
⅓ cup (80 ml) tamarind juice (page 29)
1–3 tablespoons coarsely chopped dried chilies depending on how spicy you want the dish
Kaffir lime leaves, thinly julienned, for garnish

Soak the glass vermicelli in water for half an hour. Then drain and set aside.

While the noodles are soaking, stir-fry the shrimp in unscented oil until pink. Remove and set aside.

Add more cooking oil and the shallots to the pan and stir-fry until the shallots turned opaque. Set aside.

Pour 1 cup of the coconut milk into a pot, then season with the palm sugar, fish sauce and tamarind juice. Mix and heat until boiling, stirring occasionally. Set aside and reserve for later use.

"Stir-fry" the drained glass vermicelli in the remaining 1 cup coconut milk, cooked for about 5–7 minutes. Add the reserved cup of seasoned coconut milk.

Add the shrimp and shallots, leaving some shallots for garnish. Add the chilies. Stir-fry until dry and the noodles are cooked through.

Scatter the julienned kaffir lime leaves and remaining shallots over the top as garnish.

A Family Food Gathering in Hua Hin

There is real New Year, which happens on January 1 every year. There is the Chinese New Year, which marks the start of the lunar new year. Luckily for Thais, we have a third New Year: Songkhran, which takes place every year on April 13. Around this time of year, business basically slows to a halt for at least a week or two, and sometimes for a month, as it is typically considered the Thai "summer," and is the hottest time of the year.

Every April 13 starts the same way for us, at 5 a.m. in the morning in Hua Hin. My husband's family has a family compound next to the beach, on land gifted many years ago to their ancestor by King Rama V. That ancestor, Somdet Chao Phraya Borom Maha Pichaiyat, had seven wives and 35 children, and every one of those children has a residence on this beachside parcel of land named after the family patriarch, "Baan Pichaiyat."

Because my parents went to school with Win's parents, aunts and uncles, I remember staying at Baan Pichaiyat as a kid, dealing cards with my future husband's cousins and trying to play soccer on the beach at low tide. We played "bullshit" in the hallways, forcing our parents to step over us on their way to the buffet table. We pushed our luck with tennis when the heat wasn't overpowering. We ate rice and omelets when we got hungry, doused with plenty of Maggi Seasoning, and I talked everyone's ears off with my Michael Jackson trivia. No one cared that I wore glasses and had a mullet.

Now when I see those cousins, they have kids of their own, and we never play those games anymore. But we still see each other every year in our customary purple, worn to commemorate Chao Phraya Pichaiyat's birthday, Saturday. We make merit at the crack of dawn with a procession of 20 monks who pass down the road that runs through the compound like an artery, bypassing the shrine devoted to the family patriarch before ending abruptly at the sea.

The setting is the same, but the food is better. Before the monks arrive, we get *patongko* (deep-fried Chinese-style crullers) drizzled with condensed milk and thick, strong cups of hot coffee. After the alms-giving, we gorge ourselves on fermented rice noodles in beef curry and rice topped with a Chinese-style chicken gravy garnished with a sunny-side up fried egg. Perhaps most importantly, we remember the family legacy via a few special recipes gleaned from the recipe archives, such as the *gang massaman* (Massaman curry), a dish that family members say first came to Thailand via Pichaiyat's ancestor Sheikh Ahmad.

Gang Som Southern Fish Curry

This is not a traditional sour curry recipe. It's taken from the Bunnag family recipe archive, where it is referred to as *gang som chak*. This *gang som* resembles regular sour curry, except that the chili paste base includes kaffir lime peel, lemongrass and galangal, much like *gang ped* or *gang kua* (red curry). This curry makes a lot of use of morning glory (but not the Chinese kind, because it doesn't keep its shape after long cooking). The protein is a white-fleshed fish; if you were to use three-layer pork or fatty pork, the name of this dish would be "*taypoe* pork curry." The three flavors featured here are sour (hence the name), salty, and sweet (it's a Central Thai family, after all). Speaking of which, you can add coconut milk to this, and it will be delicious in a different way.

SERVES 6 ◦ **PREP TIME: 35 MINUTES** ◦ **COOKING TIME: 20 MINUTES**

4–8 dried chilies, depending on your spice tolerance
1 teaspoon minced galangal
4 tablespoons minced lemongrass, tender inner part of bottom third only
4 tablespoons minced shallots
2 tablespoons minced garlic
1 teaspoon grated kaffir lime rind
1 teaspoon shrimp paste (*kapi*)
1 teaspoon salt
2–3 tablespoons unscented oil (vegetable oil)
2 lbs (1 kg) fatty, white-fleshed fish, flesh cut into bite-sized pieces
6 cups (1.5 l) water
3 tablespoons sugar, or to taste
3 tablespoons fish sauce, or to taste
3 tablespoons tamarind juice (page 29), or to taste
Salt, to taste
8 oz (240 g) Thai morning glory, or spinach
6–8 kaffir lime leaves, shredded
Juice of 1 kaffir lime (regular lime may be substituted)
3–4 tablespoons coconut milk (optional)
Serve with lime wedges, Nam Pla Prik (page 30) and steamed rice

Pound the chilies, galangal, lemongrass, shallots, garlic, kaffir lime rind, shrimp paste and salt into an even paste in a mortar and pestle.

In unscented oil in a soup pot over medium heat, fry the paste until aromatic (about 1 minute). Add the fish and fry until cooked through, adding a little water as you go along if necessary.

Add the water, sugar, fish sauce, tamarind juice and salt to taste. After it starts boiling, add the morning glory (or spinach) and kaffir lime leaves and juice. Taste to check the seasoning and adjust as necessary.

If you are using coconut milk, now is when you want to add a dash or two. Allow to simmer for about 10–15 minutes for the flavors to meld. Serve with steamed rice, Nam Pla Prik and lime wedges.

Why Phuket's Cuisine is Unlike Any Other

Once upon a time, a town rose up out of an island, famed for its valuable reserves of tin. Home to a tin mining boom from the 1850s to the 1900s, Phuket became a bustling trading port luring visitors from all reaches of Asia, particularly Hokkien Chinese from Fujian province via nearby Penang. What resulted was a melting pot: a stew of local Southern Thais, local Thai-Muslims, Malay neighbors and immigrating Hokkien Chinese, all of whom melded together to create literal stews of their own.

What I am attempting to describe is a unique food scene built on the foundations of a community unlike anything anywhere else. The unrestrained fire of Southern Thailand melded with the heady spices of Malaysia and culinary artistry of the Hokkien Chinese, some of the finest cooks in the region. The dishes that were born, many of which are still sold on the street, feature different combinations of these elements and, to this writer's mind at least, represent some of the most underrated dishes in Thailand.

Recipes for some of the most famous of these dishes follow. Sadly, we are unable to get to them all. Those overlooked dishes include *ang-su*, a dessert of sticky rice flour, nuts and sugar, and *o-aew*, a handmade jelly of bananas and Taiwanese fig seeds that takes eight hours to set before it is loaded with shaved ice, bananas, and a sweet red syrup. And perhaps most famously, the special snack known as *o-tao*, a thin crispy crepe of flour and egg topped with taro, oysters, onion, garlic and deep-fried pork rinds, seasoned with soy sauce and served hot off the griddle from a vendor in Phuket's very own Chinatown. Hopefully, you will be inspired enough by this book to brave a trip to Phuket someday on your own.

Phuket Steamed Fish Balls

Little did I realize that big steamed fish balls were a thing in Phuket, particularly for breakfast or lunch. We went to the original place that created them, a Chinese restaurant called Laem Thong in Phuket Town. There, they make their fishballs out of 100 percent leftover white fish trimmings, without any flour. The balls were huge, about the size of a child's fist, festooned with fresh coriander leaves (cilantro), Thai celery and deep-fried garlic. The dipping sauce (there is always a dipping sauce) is the standard seafood dipping sauce (recipe on page 33). Because Laem Thong is about to close (no one in the younger generation wants to take it on), I thought I'd include this recipe as an example of an heirloom-quality Phuket dish that's become increasingly harder to find.

SERVES 4 ● PREP TIME 1 HOUR (INCLUDES 30 MINUTE REST TIME) ● COOKING TIME: 15 MINUTES

1 lb (500 g) firm white fish like cod, halibut or hake, skinned and cut into filets
1 tablespoon salt
2 tablespoons tapioca starch
½ teaspoon baking powder
1 teaspoon white pepper
3 Thai celery stalks, chopped (or the leaves of a celery plant)
3 tablespoons deep-fried garlic slivers
Handful of fresh coriander leaves (cilantro)

In a blender or food processor, blitz the white fish until it becomes a fine paste. With a spatula, scrape down the sides and blitz again with the salt, tapioca, baking powder and pepper until well blended.

Transfer the fish paste to a cutting board. With wet hands, knead the fish paste well, slapping it onto the board a couple of times. This makes the paste springy. Wrap the paste in plastic wrap and put it in the freezer for 30 minutes.

After half an hour, take it out of the freezer. It should firmed up well. Wet your hands with some water and take a big spoonful of the fish paste onto your palm and shape into a ball. Repeat until all the fish paste is used up.

In a pot of barely boiling water, add the fish balls and boil them carefully for about 15 minutes. They will puff up and double in size. Once cooked, put them in a strainer and stop the cooking process by dunking them in a bowl of iced water.

Drain and serve with your Thai seafood dipping sauce, a garnish of Thai celery leaves and deep-fried garlic, and fresh coriander leaves.

Hokkien Fried Noodles

One of the dishes that most betrays Phuket's Hokkien Chinese influence is this delicious bowl of noodles. Unlike the Malaysian version, we add a fried egg on top (sunny-side up with a runny yolk, please!) and deep-fried pork rinds.

SERVES 4 ◦ PREP TIME: 45 MINUTES ◦ COOKING TIME: 15 MINUTES

⅓ lb (150 g) pork shoulder, thinly sliced

⅓ lb (80 g) pork liver, sliced ½ inch (12.5 mm) thick

¼ teaspoon salt

1 teaspoon light soy sauce

2 tablespoons Chinese rice wine

2 teaspoons cornstarch

6 big whole prawns (8 oz/200 g) peeled and deveined with tails left on (reserve heads and shells)

½ teaspoon salt

¼ teaspoon baking powder

1 packet or roughly 14 oz (400 g) Hokkien yellow noodles (can substitute udon noodles)

2 tablespoons lard or vegetable oil

1 inch (2.5 cm) ginger, peeled and sliced into thin slivers

4 cloves garlic, coarsely chopped

1 teaspoon finely sliced deseeded finger-length chili or chili powder (*prik pon*)

¾ cup (200 ml) chicken stock (or water with a little stock cube)

1 cup (80 g) green cabbage, cut into ½ inch (1.25 cm) wide slices

2 green onions (scallions), cut into 1 inch (2.5 cm) pieces

A grind or two of cracked peppercorns, or to taste

4 sunny-side up eggs with runny yolk, as topping

Deep-fried Pork Rinds (recipe on facing page)

Sriracha Chili Sauce (page 31), to taste

Sauce

1 tablespoon oyster sauce

1½ teaspoons light soy sauce

2½ tablespoons thick soy sauce

½ teaspoon sesame oil

Make the **Sauce** by mixing all the ingredients together in a small bowl before you start cooking. Set aside.

Prepare the pork shoulder and liver. It's easier to slice when the meat is slightly frozen. Season with the salt, soy sauce and rice wine. Mix well. Add the cornstarch and mix again. Set aside for at least 10 minutes while continuing to prep.

Wash and dry the prawns. Remove the head, pull off the tail and peel off the shell and legs. Reserve the shells and heads. Devein the prawns by cutting a slit into the rounded side and removing the black vein. Sprinkle with the salt and the baking powder and mix thoroughly. Leave to marinate for 10–30 minutes.

Wash the noodles in 2 changes of water and drain in a colander.

Heat the lard or vegetable oil in a wok. Add the reserved prawn heads and shells and fry for a minute to infuse the oil. Remove and discard the prawn heads and shells. If the shells soaked up some

of the lard, add a little more lard to the wok.

Make sure the lard is hot, then quickly fry the prawns to just cook them. The time for this will depend on the thickness and temperature of the prawns, but will rarely be more than two minutes. Remove and set aside.

Check that the lard is smoking hot, then add the ginger. Stir and immediately add the garlic. As soon as the garlic takes the lightest

Deep-fried Pork Rinds

PREP TIME: 30 MINUTES
COOKING TIME: 1.5 HOURS

500 g (1 lb) pork skin, cut into
    2-inch (5-cm) pieces
2 cups (500 ml) vegetable oil or
    other unscented oil
2 tablespoons sea salt

Bring some salted water to a boil in a saucepan and blanch the pork skin. Reduce the heat to low and simmer the pork skin in the water for 20 minutes.

Remove the pork skin from the water and pat dry. The drier the pork skin, the better.

Set the oven to 140°C (285°F). Place the pork skin on a metal rack on a lined oven tray to dry for 1 hour.

Take the pork skin out of the oven, heat the vegetable oil to 180°C (355°F) and deep fry them in batches, 1–2 minutes each batch, until the pieces are fluffy and crisp.

Remove to drain on a platter lined with paper towels. Season with sea salt and serve.

bit of color, add the meat and liver and give them a quick stir. Spread the meat and liver out flat in the wok and let it sear for 30 to 60 seconds before stirring again.

When the meat is completely cooked and slightly brown, add the noodles and chilies and stir to mix.

Pour in the Sauce and toss to coat as evenly as you can, then add the stock and mix. Leave at full heat to boil until reduced, stirring occasionally. This should take no

more than 3 minutes. The Sauce will become dark and shiny as it reduces.

Add the cabbage and stir about a minute until the cabbage just starts to wilt. Turn off the heat and add the prawns and green onions (reserve some for garnish).

Add the black pepper and adjust seasoning as needed. Serve right away with the fried eggs, pork rinds and Sriracha Chili Sauce.

Moo Hong Braised Pork Belly

This Phuket favorite is a braised pork belly in a dark and aromatic sauce. It's most reminiscent of the Chinese red pork belly (*hong shao rou*) except there's no initial blanching step and no Chinese wine in the sauce. I'm sure those things would be welcome additions, but this recipe is the pared-back Southern Thai version.

SERVES 6 • PREP TIME: 1 HOUR 20 MINUTES AND UP TO 3–4 HOURS • COOKING TIME: UP TO 3-4 HOURS

2 tablespoons chopped garlic
4 coriander (cilantro) root, chopped
1 tablespoon black peppercorns
3 tablespoons shaved palm sugar
2 cups (500 ml) and 1 tablespoon unscented oil
2 lbs (approx 1 kg) pork belly, cut into bite-sized pieces
2 tablespoons soy sauce
2 tablespoons dark soy sauce
2 tablespoons oyster sauce
3 star anise
2 teaspoons salt, to taste
Fresh coriander leaves (cilantro), to serve

In a mortar and pestle, pound the garlic, coriander root, peppercorns and palm sugar into a paste. Set aside.

In a deep-bottomed pan or wok, heat 2 cups of oil and fry the pork belly in batches until the pork takes on a light caramel color. (Be very careful, the oil will spatter. Place a lid over the top of the pan while frying the pork). Remove and set aside.

In another pot, heat the remaining 1 tablespoon of oil and add the paste. Heat to "sprout" the paste until aromatic and saucy. Once the sugar melts, add the pork and stir until the pork is covered with the sauce. Add enough water to the pot to just cover the pork pieces. Stir.

Add both the soy sauces, oyster sauce and star anise. Bring to a boil, then cover with a lid and bring to a simmer. Check periodically to ensure the water level isn't too low and add more water every so often to make it saucy but still thick.

After at least an hour, the pork should be soft and the sauce thick. If you like the pork to be truly tender, simmer over low heat for a few more hours. Do not forget to check the water level.

Add the salt to taste and garnished with the fresh coriander leaves. Serve with steamed white rice.

Phuket-style Fluffy Omelet (inspired by Raya Restaurant)

This recipe is inspired by the fluffy, pork rind-strewn omelet served at Raya Restaurant in Phuket town, one of the island's most revered restaurants. It is considered Hokkien-style cooking, unlike much of the Thai mainland, where Teochew Chinese cuisine usually reigns supreme. You will need a deep saucepan to cook the omelet in, as well as a fine-meshed sieve. Two wooden cooking spoons are also recommended.

SERVES 2 • PREP TIME: 5 MINUTES • COOKING TIME: 5 MINUTES

1 cup (250 ml) unscented cooking
    oil (vegetable oil is best)
2 eggs
1 teaspoon fish sauce
Deep-fry Pork Rinds (for garnish,
    optional, recipe on page 131)
Sriracha Chili Sauce (as accompani-
    ment, recipe on page 31)

In a saucepan, heat the oil over high heat.

Beat the eggs with a fork until frothy, and add the fish sauce. Beat well again.

With your fork, add a few drops of the egg to the oil to test. If the egg drops immediately bubble up like the villain in an acid bath in a James Bond movie, the oil is ready to go. Remove the egg bubbles from the oil.

Position your sieve over the hot oil and drizzle the beaten egg mixture over it. The egg bits will immediately bubble as they hit the oil, so I recommend moving your sieve around so that the drizzles will form an interesting pattern, like a funnel cake. Once most of the egg mixture has gone through the sieve (some of the froth will remain), set your sieve aside and concentrate on your omelet.

Keep the sides of the omelet free from the edges of the pan with your wooden spoon, checking pe-riodically after 30 seconds into the cooking process to see if the omelet is an appropriate golden-brown color underneath. Once it reaches that color, carefully turn your om-elet over in the oil using your two wooden spoons.

Keep an eye on your omelet so that it doesn't burn, checking the underside of the omelet from time to time. After 30 seconds to 1 minute, it should also be golden brown. You can turn it over to cook again to ensure your omelet is extremely crispy, or you can now remove the omelet to a cooling rack set over a baking sheet. The omelet will deflate slightly as it cools. To make the omelet as Phuket-ish as possible, you can scatter pork rinds over the top.

Serve your omelet as soon as you can with freshly steamed white jasmine rice and a side of Sriracha Chili Sauce. This omelet also goes well with spicy curries, to mitigate the heat.

The Muslim Community in Southern Thailand

Muslims have lived in Thailand since the 13th century when, as the kingdom of Siam, it was known as a land of religious tolerance. Since then, Thai Muslims have formed communities throughout the country, from peaceful enclaves in the North to making up the majority of people in the far South.

Arab traders who plied their trade along what is now Southern Thailand and Northern Malaysia first brought Islam to Thailand. Later, in the 1890s, the kingdom annexed what was formerly the Pattani Kingdom, officially incorporating them into Thailand in 1902. All the while, the people have retained their own cultural identity, speaking a language particular to only that region called Tawi and developing a unique cuisine made up of Chinese, Thai and Malay influences. Today, at around 8 percent of the population, Muslims are the biggest religious minority in Thailand, and more than 3,000 mosques pepper the country, with the majority located in the province of Pattani.

Since 2001, the three southernmost provinces of Pattani, Narathiwat and Yala have been the site of a simmering insurgency driven by the people's deep connection to a Malay identity rather than to a Thai one. This unrest has not come without a high cost: There have been more than 3,000 deaths since 2003, the result of crackdowns spearheaded by deposed Prime Minister Thaksin Shinawatra.

Today, some Muslims in the South balk at being called Thai Muslims, preferring instead to identify as "Malayu," or Malay Muslims. The gap between this community with the rest of Thailand has been exacerbated by the relative poverty of the deep South in comparison with much of the rest of Thailand.

Unlike in the far South, where 90 percent of the people in the three southernmost provinces are Muslim, the Thai Muslim communities in the North have intermarried and assimilated more into the majority Thai Buddhist population. The smaller numbers of Muslims may have contributed to this, as does their ethnic makeup; Northern Thai Muslim communities seem mostly descended from Chin Haw, or Chinese Muslims, credited with bringing *khao soy* (curried Northern Thai noodles) to Northern Thailand. In the East, Muslim Chams migrated from neighboring Vietnam and Cambodia, living in Thailand since the 15th century.

Despite the fractious relationship between the Muslims of Southern Thailand and the Thai government, no one disputes the remarkable contributions of the Thai Muslim community to the country's cuisine. From crowd-pleasing biryanis and sinus-clearing soups to flaky roti and toothsome curries, Thai food would be nowhere as good as it is without the flavors of the far South.

Thai Oxtail Soup

This dish can be eaten alone, but I like it paired with the Thai-style Chicken Biryani (page 138). Unlike the oxtail stews of the West, this soup is tart, fiery and strangely refreshing.

SERVES 6 ⸱ TOTAL PREP TIME 20 MINUTES ⸱ COOKING TIME: 2–3 HOURS (A PRESSURE COOKER OR CROCK POT CAN BE USED TO SAVE COOKING TIME).

2 lbs (1 kg) oxtail
7 cups (1.75 l) water
3 coriander (cilantro) root, bruised
½ tablespoon cardamom pods
1 star anise
1 stick cinnamon
2–3 cloves
2-inch (5-cm) piece ginger, peeled and sliced
1 teaspoon whole peppercorns
5 bird's eye chilies or finger-length chilies (*prik chee fah*), bruised
½ teaspoon coriander seeds
1 onion, sliced
½ tablespoon salt
1 cup (150 g) cherry tomatoes
3 key limes quartered (optional is using Persian limes as the flavor may be too bitter, just squeeze extra juice at the end)
1 stalk Thai celery, chopped (can use Western celery leaves)
Salt, to taste
Fish sauce, to taste
Deep-fried shallots, for garnish
3 limes, cut into wedges, for garnish
Sliced bird's eye chilies, for garnish
Coriander leaves (cilantro), for garnish

Heat a large heavy bottom pot until hot. Add the oxtail and dry roast until the sides are browned. To prevent burning, you can add a little water to the bottom of the pot. Add the water, coriander root, cardamom, star anise, cinnamon, cloves, ginger, peppercorns, chilies and coriander seeds. Cover and simmer on low heat for 2½–3 hours, skimming off any fat and scum that floats to the top.

Remove from the heat and strain the broth into another pot. If it is fatty, try straining it through a dish towel that has been soaked in cold water and rung out. You can also place the broth in the fridge for a few hours and then scrape the solidified fat layer off the top.

Return the strained broth back to the first pot, skimming any remaining fat that floats to the top.

Add the onion, salt and tomatoes. Bring back to a simmer and boil until the onions are soft and tomatoes have lost their shape a bit, about 25 minutes. Add the limes and celery. Taste and adjust seasoning with more salt or fish sauce.

Serve garnished with deep-fried shallots, lime wedges, sliced chilies and coriander leaves.

Massaman Curry

The origin of this curry (the name means "Muslim curry"), remains murky. The only thing everyone agrees on is that it isn't typically Thai. Some people say it came from Persia; others say it came from Malaysia. Some people who lean toward it being from Persia—including my husband's family—say, predictably, that the Bunnag's family founder Sheikh Ahmad brought the recipe (originally a lamb stew flavored with pomegranate molasses) to Siamese shores more than 400 years ago.

SERVES 6 ● PREP TIME: 20 MINUTES, TOTAL COOK TIME 1:15 MINUTES ● COOKING TIME: 1 HOUR

Curry Paste

10–15 long Thai chilies (*prik diiplii*) (these are sun dried & mild) or ½–¾ cup (35 g) dried red chilies, seeds taken out and cut into small pieces

1 teaspoon black peppercorns

½ teaspoon each of mace, cloves and cardamom seeds

1 tablespoon cumin seeds

2 tablespoons coriander seeds

½ teaspoon nutmeg

2 large shallots or ½ cup (52 g) Thai shallots

8 cloves garlic or ½ cup (85 g) Thai garlic

1 tablespoon coriander (cilantro) root, minced

3 tablespoons thinly sliced lemon-grass, tender inner part of bottom third only

1 inch (2.5 cm) knob of galangal, peeled and sliced

1 teaspoon shrimp paste (*kapi*), wrapped in aluminum foil and heated gently until fragrant

Chicken Massaman Curry

1 cup (250 ml) coconut cream (called *hua kati* or coconut head)

4–5 lbs (2 kgs) chicken, cut into 16 pieces

4 cups (1 l) coconut milk (called *hang kati* or coconut tail)

12 pearl onions, peeled

12 small potatoes or 3 large potatoes, peeled and cut into 4 pieces each

½ cup (75 g) raisins

¼ cup (60 g) roasted peanuts

2 tablespoons fish sauce, or to taste

1 tablespoon shaved palm sugar, or to taste

1 tablespoon tamarind juice (page 29), or to taste

2 tablespoons bitter orange (*som saa*) juice (a half and half mix of lime and orange juice may be substituted)

Red finger-length chilies, sliced, for garnish (optional)

Coriander leaves (cilantro), for garnish

Whole roasted peanuts, for garnish

Make the **Curry Paste** by dry roasting the chilies, peppercorns, mace, cloves, cardamom seeds, cumin and coriander seeds in an oven or on a hot pan until aromatic (about 3–5 minutes).

Place the toasted chili spice mixture in a mortar and pestle and pound until ground then add the nutmeg. Continue to grind to a fine spice blend. A food processor or spice grinder may be used.

Next dry roast the shallots and garlic, with skins on, in either a pan or oven until the insides are soft. Remove the skins and add the shallots, garlic, coriander root, lemongrass, galangal and shrimp paste to the mortar. Continue pounding until a paste is formed.

Make the **Chicken Massaman Curry**. In a large pot over medium-high heat, heat the coconut cream until it "breaks": when dots of oil appear on the surface of the cream (or when it is reduced by a third). Add the Curry Paste and fry together until aromatic, about 2–4 minutes.

Add the chicken and cook over medium heat until the chicken is partially cooked, approximately 5 more minutes. Add the coconut milk, pearl onions, potatoes, raisins, peanuts, fish sauce, palm sugar and tamarind juice.

Simmer until the chicken and potatoes are just cooked through. Add the bitter orange juice (*som saa*). Taste again to adjust seasoning.

Serve with steamed rice. Garnish with fresh sliced red chilies, coriander leaves and roasted peanuts.

Thai-style Chicken Biryani

This dish, adapted from the Indians, is commonly known as *khao mok gai*, or "chicken buried under a mountain of rice." However, the recipe here is called *khao buree* (or "cigarette" or "smoked" rice) and, as another entry from the Bunnag family cookbook, is served at most family gatherings. It's quite labor-intensive, but has been simplified considerably (!) from the original recipe, which calls for the making of a lid and oven-proof bowl from dough.

SERVES 8 ● PREP TIME: APPROX 2½ HOURS ● COOKING TIME: APPROX 2 HOURS

An "old" or mature chicken, about
    4½ lbs (2 kgs)
10 small potatoes, peeled
Several pieces of natural wood
    charcoal or wood embers for
    smoking. (Note: do not use
    "pressed" charcoal that contains
    chemicals)
¾ cup (75 g) thinly sliced shallots
1⅓ cups (300 g) ghee
Heat proof bowl/ramekin
Deep-fried shallots for garnish
    (optional)
Pickled Cucumbers (see facing
    page), to serve

Marinade
2 tablespoons peeled garlic
2 tablespoons finely chopped ginger
6 red finger-length chilies (*prik chee
    fah*, if available)
3 tablespoons salt
3 tablespoons sugar
9 tablespoons Garam Masala (you
    can buy ready-made or make
    your own, recipe on facing page)
2 cups (500 g) plain yogurt
1 cup (40 g) finely sliced mint leaves
    (reserved half for garnish)

Rice
5 cloves
3 cinnamon sticks
6 cardamom pods
4 cups (900 g) uncooked jasmine rice
Pinch of saffron

Cut the chicken into 10 pieces (2 pieces per leg—thigh and drumstick; breast, 2 pieces per side; wings with back attached, 2 pieces). Put them in a large dish.

    Prepare the **Marinade**. In a mortar and pestle or food processor, pound the garlic, ginger and chilies into a paste.

Massage this paste into the chicken pieces together with the salt, sugar, Garam Masala, yogurt and half of the mint leaves. Add the potatoes. Put in the refrigerator to marinate for at least an hour.

In a heavy pan, light several pieces of natural-wood charcoal to get them to start burning.

Sauté the shallots in the ghee until crispy (5 minutes). Strain the ghee into a heat-proof bowl and reserve the shallots for later use. Using tongs, place some hot charcoal into the ghee. Cover quickly with a lid. Leave for 15–20 minutes to allow the smoky flavors to permeate the ghee.

In a *mor kaek* (tandoor), a Dutch oven or stock pot place the marinated chicken and potatoes. Place onto the stove over medium heat with the lid on. Cook for 15 minutes, stirring occasionally until the liquid has mostly evaporated.

While the chicken is cooking, start cooking the **Rice**. Fill a medium to large pot halfway with water and place on the stove. Add the cloves, cinnamon and cardamom and turn to high heat.

Wash, rinse and drain the rice 3–4 times until the water becomes clear. Add the rice to the pot once the water is boiling, and cook for 5 minutes. Pour the rice into a colander to drain the water. Add a pinch of saffron to the rice and mix in.

Scoop the drained rice and aromatics over the chicken in the Dutch oven and spread out evenly.

Strain the ghee through a fine-mesh sieve to remove the charcoal. Add all but 2 tablespoons of the

ghee evenly over the rice, and save the charcoal and reserved ghee for later use.

Place a small 1½ inch (4 cm) heat proof bowl or ramekin on top of the rice. Add the ghee-soaked charcoal to the bowl and light it on fire. The ghee should readily burn, allowing the charcoal to become red-hot again. Once the ember is glowing, pour the reserved ghee onto the charcoal to create smoke. Quickly place a lid or aluminum foil onto the Dutch oven/baking dish to trap the smoke.

Place into a oven preheated to 325° F (160° C) for 35–40 minutes.

Check that the chicken is fully cooked. Remove the bowl with charcoal. With a fork fluff the top of the rice. Assemble the rice and chicken onto a serving platter with the remaining thinly sliced mint leaves and crispy shallots, if using. Serve with the Pickled Cucumbers.

Garam Masala

This is actually one of three (!) garam masala recipes in the family cookbook. Since the other two recipes yield such huge quantities of spice, I opted for this one.

4 tablespoons cumin powder
3 tablespoons cinnamon powder
1 tablespoon clove powder
1 tablespoon cardamom powder

Combine all and mix well.

Pickled Cucumbers

10 mini cucumbers, cut in half vertically and each piece cut in half horizontally to form spears
2 tablespoons ginger, finely julienned
2 tablespoons red shallots, thinly sliced
1 each green, orange and red finger-length chilies, seeds scraped out and thinly sliced
½ cup (125 ml) white vinegar
½ cup (100 g) sugar
1 teaspoon salt

Arrange the cucumber spears in a pan big enough to hold them all and scatter the ginger, shallots and chilies over the top.

Mix the vinegar, salt, and sugar together in a small saucepan. Heat over medium heat until it comes to a low boil. Wait for the sugar and salt to dissolve before turning off the heat. Allow to cool.

Pour the vinegar mixture over the cucumbers and cover. Keep in a cool and dry place. Leave to pickle for at least 2 hours. Serve on the side with the Chicken Biryani.

CHAPTER 6
Thai Drinks and Desserts

Pioneers of the Sweet and Savory

For centuries, Thai desserts have pushed the boundary between sweet and savory. Often it's just a case of what ingredients are on hand: Rice, rice flour, palm sugar, coconut, all of which boast rounded, supple flavors which don't lean too far out into the realm of the saccharine-sweet. This cannot be a surprise for any long-time disciple of the food of Thailand, which most famously characterizes its cuisine as a balance between five flavors. After all, it means a lot when the sweetest traditional desserts in Thai cuisine—the "golden" trilogy of *foy tong*, *tong yip*, and *tong yod*—are actually Portuguese imports.

In a country where curries are described as "sweet" (*gang kiew waan*, or "sweet green curry") and palm sugar plays a big role in chili dips, Thailand's willingness to blur the lines between the main course and the final act is not a fad, but a tradition (although traditionalists will be quick to point out that "sweet green curry" refers to the color of the curry, and not the flavor). In fact, in the olden days, Thai dishes were served all at the same time, not in courses, meaning that what people today would think of as desserts were placed on the table right alongside appetizers and mains, with diners free to pick from whatever they fancied at the moment.

It's a little surprise, then, that Thai palates even today remain more sophisticated when it comes to their snacks and desserts, incorporating hints of funk into concoctions that would normally skew purely citrus or sugary. Shredded shrimp or fish are actually candied and wrapped up into cookie-like shells lined in meringue (*kanom bueng*) or used to top sticky rice coated in a salty-sweet coconut cream (*khao niew moon*). Shallots are fried until brown and sweet, topping a coconut custard where the sweetness echoes the flavors of the shallots (*kanom maw gang*).

But the biggest ingredient playing on both sides of the sweet-savory divide is coconut milk, used liberally to slather over sticky rice, as a salty top layer over a pan of sweet jello, or as a "broth" in which rice flour dumplings or boiled bananas are set afloat. In fact, the latter make up the earliest types of Thai desserts, and as such, demonstrate the widest variety of local sweets available.

Gluay Buad Chee Bananas in Sweet Coconut Cream

In Thailand we use *gluay nam wah* for this recipe. It is less sweet and firmer than *gluay hom* (regular Western bananas). If using Western bananas, they will cook faster.

SERVES 4 ⬦ PREP TIME 10 MINUTES ⬦ COOKING TIME: 20 MINUTES

4 cups (1 l) coconut milk
¼ cup (50 g) shaved palm sugar
½ cup (100 g) sugar
1 teaspoon salt
3 cups (900 g) firm bananas, peeled and cut into 3-inch (7.5-cm) chunks

In a saucepan, combine the coconut milk, both types of sugar and the salt. Bring to a boil over medium-high heat. Lower the heat to simmer and let the favors meld for about 5 minutes. It should taste sweet with a little bit of salt.

Add the banana chunks and bring to a boil again. Taste for seasoning and add more sugar and/or salt if necessary.

Lower the heat to simmer and cook for about 10 minutes or until the bananas are softened. They should be coated in the sauce.

Turn off the heat and serve in a bowl at room temperature.

Khao Niew Mamuang Mango Sticky Rice

When you make this recipe, the pleasure in eating it increases exponentially with the ripeness of the mango (duh!) or other fruit, as well as the crispy mung bean topping, which I'd argue is even more integral than the coconut cream topping. The textural contrast is just that important to me.

SERVES: 4 ● PREP TIME: 1 HOUR PLUS 2–24 HOUR SOAK TIME FOR STICKY RICE ● COOKING TIME: 30 MINUTES

Sticky Rice (Khao Niew Moon)

3 cups (600 g) uncooked sticky rice (*khao niew*)
1 cup (250 ml) coconut cream
½ cup (100 g) sugar
1 tablespoon salt

Coconut Cream Topping

1½ cups (375 ml) coconut cream
1 teaspoon salt (or to taste)

Topping

3 tablespoons yellow mung beans (aka yellow mung dal), dry-roasted until crispy (toasted sesame seeds, grape nuts cereal or even cornflakes may be used as substitutes)
Mango, fresh

Make the **Coconut Cream Topping**. Heat the coconut cream and salt over very high heat. Taste and add more salt if you prefer.

To make the **Sticky Rice**, soak the sticky rice grains overnight or in hot water for at least 2 hours.

Steam the sticky rice until cooked, about 30–45 minutes. Heat the coconut cream with the sugar and salt, and stir until the sugar dissolved.

In a deep bowl, place the hot Sticky Rice and pour the coconut cream over it. Mix together until the grains are coated with the coconut cream. Cover the rice and

wait for 15 minutes, then mix the rice grains again.

To serve the rice, pour the Coconut Cream Topping on top of the rice and pepper with the dry-roasted crispy mung beans.

Pair with ripe, fresh cut mango. If you don't have mango, you can use anything sweet and slightly tart, like peaches, pineapple or even strawberries.

Aunt Priew's Halo Halo

You're right in thinking this is not a Thai dessert. In fact, it's Filipino. My Aunt Priew learned this recipe from her years living in Manila during her husband's tenure at the Asian Development Bank. Since then, she has served a (very simplified and less traditionally sweet) version of this dessert at every big family gathering at her house. The very look of it makes me smile.

SERVES 6 ⦿ PREP TIME: 10 MINUTES ⦿ COOKING TIME: 5 MINUTES

2–3 fresh bananas (2 if using Western bananas), sliced

6 jackfruit, chopped (if you can't find fresh or canned jackfruit, use pineapple)

1 jar drained nata de coco, a type of coconut jelly (you can find this at the Asian market)

1 can drained sugar palm seeds, chopped (you can also find this at the Asian market)

3 cups (400 g) crushed ice

One 12-oz (375-ml) can evaporated milk

Combine the first 4 ingredients in a bowl, then ladle into 6 individual bowls. Divide the crushed ice among the bowls. Pour the evaporated milk over it. You're done!

A Persian-inspired Family Favorite

Look at the face of any member of my husband's family, and you will see what you think of as a stereotypically Thai person. But within the first five minutes of any discussion on family history, you are certain to be regaled with stories of far-off Persian ancestors who traveled all the way to Asia in search of fortune and prosperity, and found all that their hearts could desire in the kingdom of Siam.

Of course, that Persian ancestor was alive many generations ago, and any hint of Middle Eastern blood is likely to fill a thimble, if that. But at family gatherings, his legacy reigns supreme. Known as Sheikh Ahmad of Qom, he was born in 1543 and traveled to Siam in 1602–1605. After marrying a local Siamese woman, he settled in the then-capital of Ayutthaya and made his fortune as a trader, enough so as to gain influence at the royal court.

He attained several government posts and eventually rose to the rank of Chao Phraya after helping King Songtham repel an attempted rebellion staged by Japanese traders. Under King Songtham, Sheikh Ahmad was eventually made the kingdom's first Muslim community leader, called the Chula Rachamontri. In 1631, he passed away at the age of 88. His tomb in Ayutthaya, erected in the 1990s on the spot where he is believed to have been buried, is still visited by family members.

Sheikh Ahmad is claimed as ancestor by several families in Thailand, including the Bunnags. On my husband's side of the family, that line from Sheikh Ahmad runs through Somdej Chao Phya Borommaha Pichaiyadh, my husband's great-grandfather, whose photo still adorns our dining room. Although Sheikh Ahmad lived centuries ago, his influence is still strong in the food served at family gatherings. *Khao buree*, a type of chicken biryani reminiscent of the Thai-Muslim dish *khao mok gai* ("chicken buried under a mound of rice"), is frequently served at these occasions, alongside vats of *khao na gai*, a Chinese-inspired dish of thick chicken gravy slathered over a dish of white rice, a nod to the family's dual Persian and Chinese roots.

But perhaps the dish most illustrative of the family's Middle Eastern roots is *sai gai*, a saffron-scented deep-fried sweet that in other lands would probably be called jalebi. Although the words *sai gai* in Thai mean "chicken's innards," the sweets' circular shape only nods in the direction of the theoretical bird's intestines. In no way do these sweets actually recall bird's innards in terms of taste. Instead, these desserts are intensely sweet and crunchy, aromatic with saffron and cardamom, and crackly like caramel on the palate.

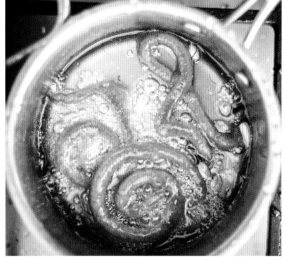

Kanom Sai Gai Saffron-scented Jalebi

Another big standard-bearer dish showcasing the Bunnag family's (distant) Persian heritage, this dessert is served at almost every big family gathering. This is a quick version made without yeast (which needs hours of rising time).

SERVES 6 ● PREP TIME: 45 MINUTES ● COOKING TIME: 15 MINUTES

1 cup (250 ml) cooking oil
1 cup (225 g) ghee

Jalebi Batter

1 cup (150 g) flour
4 tablespoons cornstarch
¼ teaspoon baking powder
½ teaspoon turmeric
4 tablespoons yogurt
⅔ cup (150 ml) water (or as much to create a pourable batter)

Syrup

1 cup (250 ml) water
2 cups (400 g) sugar
¼ teaspoon saffron
6 cardamom pods
3 cloves

Make the **Jalebi Batter**. In a bowl, mix the flour, cornstarch, baking powder, turmeric and yogurt until well incorporated. Gradually add the water, whisking until a pourable batter forms. Depending on how thick the yogurt is you may need to add additional water. Cover and set aside for 15 minutes.

Prepare the **Syrup**. In a saucepan, boil the water and mix in the sugar until it dissolves. Add the saffron, cardamom and cloves. Reduce the heat and stir occasionally until the contents take on a syrupy consistency, approximately 10–15 minutes.

In a Thai copper dessert pot or wide-mouthed pot like a wok, heat the oil and ghee together. Put the dough in a piping bag or large zip lock bag. Cut off the end leaving a very small opening or about the size of a tine of fork. A squeeze bottle may also be used. Heat the oil to medium high heat. Squeeze the dough in a circular spiral into the hot oil (or, if you are a stickler for accuracy, make into the shape of the Thai number "8" to represent "eternity"). Jalebi should puff up; if it doesn't, increase the heat. If the batter disperse in the oil as you pipe it, it is too thin and you will need to add more flour to it. If you are not able to pipe it, add a little water but always remember to add 1 teaspoon at a time until you have the desired consistency.

Fry the jalebi until crispy on both sides and when done, scoop out of the oil to drain on paper towels. Dunk right away while still hot in the saffron Syrup and leave to soak for 5 minutes. The Syrup should be medium hot to warm while you are dropping the fried jalebis. If the Syrup is too hot the jalebis will not be crisp.

Pull out and the jalebi is ready to eat. Congratulations, you have made one jalebi! Repeat the same procedure with the rest of the dough and Syrup.

Maria Guyomar de Pinha—Thailand's Escoffier

The story of the woman who would later be called "Thailand's Escoffier" seems tailor-made for a food-focused mini-series featuring a beautiful woman who is also an amazing cook. What more could anyone want? Call me, Netflix.

The real story behind Thailand's Escoffier is told through historical records, which say that she was born Maria Guyomar de Pinha in the 17th century to a Bengali-Portuguese-Japanese father named Fanik Guyomar and a Japanese mother named Ursula Yamada, whose family had fled Japan earlier to escape persecution for being Christians. The Kingdom of Siam was known as a religiously tolerant place, and Maria's family settled in Ayutthaya, the political center at that time.

Maria had the good fortune to be born during the reign of King Narai (1656–1688), who was known for being friendly to foreigners. Known as "King Narai the Great," he was the last of the Prasat Thong (loosely translating to "Golden Palace") monarchs and a big advocate for trade and diplomatic relations with foreign powers. Indeed, he opened the kingdom to such an extent that the court was full of French officials, ruffling the feathers of the local courtiers.

In 1682, Maria married Constantine Phaulkon, a Greek merchant/interpreter who spoke six languages, including Thai. This likely helped to endear him to King Narai, who eventually promoted him to a high level in his government. Eventually reaching the rank of prime councillor and winning the title of "Chao Phraya" (Lord), Phaulkon converted to Catholicism to marry Maria. They settled in a home called Baan Vichayen in Lopburi and had two children.

Unfortunately, their matrimonial bliss was short-lived. In 1688, the Siamese Revolution put an end to King Narai's reign, and the new king Phetracha was installed as head of the kingdom. Despite assurances from the French that they would protect her (after all, she was ennobled as a countess of France), she was handed over to King Phetracha and condemned to slavery in the palace kitchens.

What was bad for Maria ended up being ultimately great for Thai cuisine, unfortunately. She is now credited with crafting a slew of Thai classics, particularly desserts. These inventions included the golden *tong* sweets based on conventual sweets, a coconut custard steamed in a pumpkin known as *sankaya fuk tong*, and a coconut custard topped with savory deep-fried shallots called *kanom maw gang*. Savory curry puffs, another creation, were flaky pastries filled with a curried meat-and/or-vegetable mixture. Thai food would not be the same without Maria Guyomar de Pinha and the Portuguese influence she brought to her cooking.

When King Phetracha died, Maria stayed on in the palace, becoming head of the kitchen. Thais today know her as "Thao Thong Kip Ma."

Sankaya Fuk Tong Pumpkin Custard

This recipe is said to have been originally created by Maria Guyomar de Pinha, otherwise known as "Thao Thong Kip Ma" to the Thais. Credited with crafting a slew of Thai classics, de Pinha lived a colorful life as the wife of a French merchant who was killed during the 1688 Siamese revolution. She was subsequently enslaved by new King Phetracha, who made her work in his kitchen until his death in 1703. This recipe is a European custard made with Thai ingredients. Because there were no ramekins at that time, de Pinha used a pumpkin. This is still served all over Thailand today.

SERVES 4 ◦ PREP TIME: 15 MINUTES ◦ COOKING TIME: 1:45–2 HOURS, ALLOW TO COOL FOR A COUPLE OF HOURS TO SET

- 1 large Thai pumpkin (kabocha squash), approx 2–3 lbs (1½ kgs), deseeded and the lid cut out, Jack-o-lantern-style
- 4 eggs plus 2 egg yolks
- 1 teaspoon vanilla extract (unless you have access to a pandanus leaf)
- ½ cup (100 g) shaved palm sugar
- ½ cup (100 g) sugar
- ½ teaspoon salt
- 1 tablespoon all-purpose flour
- 1 cup (250 ml) coconut cream

If you have a pandanus leaf, extract the essence by steeping it in hot water until aromatic. Use in place of vanilla extract.

Mix the eggs, egg yolks, vanilla or pandanus extract, sugars, salt, flour and coconut cream, whisking until the sugars dissolved completely.

Strain the mixture through a cheesecloth or fine strainer into the hollowed-out pumpkin.

Steam the pumpkin, with the lid placed next to it in a steamer. The lid will take about 10–20 minutes to cook; pierce with a knife to make sure it is soft. The pumpkin itself will take around 1 hour.

After an hour, check to see if the pumpkin flesh is soft and if a skewer inserted into the custard part comes out clean. If not, steam for another 15–30 minutes.

Remove the pumpkin. Set aside to cool and allow the custard to set. Cut into wedges and serve at room temperature.

Kanom Pui Fai Cupcakes

These cupcakes are named after the "cotton balls" that they look like when they are served at the table. They are steamed instead of baked. Traditionally, they are flavored with jasmine extract, but if that's hard to find, you can substitute with vanilla. This easy to make at home version does not have cake emulsifier in it, resulting in a slightly denser cupcake.

MAKES 6–10 CUPCAKES (DEPENDING ON SIZE OF CUPCAKE HOLDER/RAMEKIN)
PREP TIME: 15 MINUTES ● COOKING TIME: 15–20 MINUTES

2 eggs (duck eggs preferred, but chicken eggs are fine)
1 cup (200 g) sugar
1½ cups (225 g) cake flour
½ teaspoon baking powder
4 tablespoons of water
1 tablespoon lime juice
1 teaspoon vanilla extract (or 2 drops of jasmine extract)
Salt, a little pinch
Muffin tin or cupcake holders (If you have a small steamer you can use stand alone cupcake holders or ramekins)
Large steamer

Whisk the eggs until frothy and then slowly add the sugar. Continue whisking until the sugar is completely dissolved.

Sift the flour and baking powder together in a bowl and then slowly add to the egg mixture and mix well. Add the water, lime juice, vanilla or jasmine extract and salt. Mix well until very fluffy and light.

Prepare the steamer as it needs to be hot when the cupcakes go in. Prepare the cupcake holders by spritzing them with oil, then fill with the batter all the way up the holder.

Place in the steamer and steam for 15–20 minutes until the cupcake tops puff up and break open, forming cratered ridges.

Coconut Ice Cream

The recipes for both the coconut ice cream and for the sweet buns were created by my friend Chris Schultz, who is an avid home cook. Thank you Chris!

FOR 4–6 PEOPLE * PREP TIME: 10 HOURS (INCLUDING FREEZING TIME) * COOKING TIME 1 HOUR

2 cups (500 ml) coconut milk (canned) or contents of one 8 fl oz can
2 heaping teaspoons cornstarch
5 tablespoons sugar
½ teaspoon salt
2 teaspoons vanilla extract
4–6 Thai Sweet Rolls (page 152) or hot dog buns
Roasted peanuts, to garnish
Sticky Rice, page 90 (optional)
Coconut milk (optional)

Take ½ cup of the coconut milk and blend with the cornstarch to make a slurry. Set aside.

Mix the remaining coconut milk, sugar, salt and vanilla extract in a saucepan and heat over medium heat (do not let it boil). Remove from the heat and add the cornstarch slurry.

Stir/whisk until thickened (it will only thicken slightly). Cool to room temperature. Put in an airtight container and freeze for at least 3 hours until just frozen through.

Take it out, break into chunks, and put into a blender. Blend to the consistency of a milkshake, then put back into the freezer for another 6 hours or until firm.

Serve with Thai Sweet Rolls or hot dog buns. Topped with roasted peanuts. You can also serve on top of Sticky Rice, or on top of Sticky Rice inside the bun. Drizzle with leftover coconut milk if you wish.

Thai Sweet Rolls

Chris Schultz came up with this sweet roll recipe to pair with the coconut ice cream. Of course, these rolls are also nice on their own or even as hot dog buns!.

MAKES 15 ROLLS • PREP TIME: 3½ HOURS • COOKING TIME: 40 MINUTES

1 cup (250 ml) pineapple juice
1 package (2¼ teaspoons/7 g) instant yeast or dry active yeast. Instant yeast will produce a higher-rising bun. If you use active dry yeast the rising time will be about 20 minutes longer with both rises
3¼ cups (415 g) all-purpose flour
¼ cup (50 g) sugar or ⅓ cup (80 ml) honey
1 teaspoon kosher salt
1 large egg plus 2 large egg yolks (reserve the whites for the wash)
4 tablespoons unsalted butter (½ stick), at room temperature
1 tablespoon water
Honey butter (optional)—½ and ½ mixture of melted butter and honey

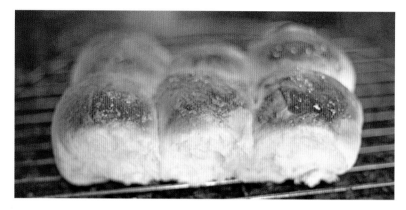

In a small saucepan, bring the pineapple juice to a simmer over medium-high heat, and cook until it has reduced to ¾ cup, about 10 minutes. Transfer the juice to a bowl or measuring cup and let cool until just warm, about 105°F (40°C). Stir in the yeast and let the mixture stand until the yeast has bloomed, about 5 minutes.

Meanwhile, in the bowl of a stand mixer with the dough hook attached, combine the flour, sugar and salt. With the mixer on low, add the yeast mixture and the egg yolks, and knead until all ingredients are incorporated. Add the butter in small pieces and continue to knead the dough, increasing speed to medium, another 5 to 10 minutes. The dough should be smooth, elastic and a little sticky. Roll the dough into a ball (no need to add extra flour). Cover the bowl with plastic wrap or a towel and set aside to rise in a warm place until doubled, about 2 hours.

Butter a 9-inch-by-13-inch (23 cm x 33 cm) baking pan. Gently tip the dough out onto a work

surface. Divide the dough into 15 equal pieces. Roll each piece into a ball and place in the prepared pan. Repeat with the remaining dough. Dough can also be rolled into elongated shape if a hot dog roll is preferred. Cover the tray lightly with plastic wrap and set aside to double again, approximately 1 hour. The dough should look puffy and spring back slowly when pressed gently.

Whisk with a fork the 2 reserved egg whites and add 1 tablespoon water. Brush the tops of the rolls with the egg white mixture before placing in the oven.

Heat the oven to 350°F (175°C). Bake until puffed and golden, about 20 minutes. Remove from the oven and brush the rolls with melted honey butter and cool on a wire rack for 20 minutes. Rolls are best eaten the same day.

The Story of the Thai Ice Cream Sandwich

In these increasingly politically divided times, it might seem impossible to bridge the chasm between the politically liberal and conservatively hidebound portions of society. Luckily, Thais have a cure for this, and that is the ice cream sandwich.

Two or, usually, three scoops of coconut ice cream, most probably studded with bits of jackfruit and jellied water chestnut, are nestled in what would appear to be a hot dog bun, split open to accommodate these melting globes of goodness. Condensed milk is drizzled on top for good measure. If you want to be fancy, you might get a few *luk chit* (sweet Asian plum seeds) tossed on top and clumps of coconut sticky rice on the bottom. It's a sandwich fit for a Dairy Queen.

These ice cream sandwiches are beloved by all Thais, from all echelons of society, so it's no surprise, then, that street vendors can be found throughout Bangkok's side-streets, selling their wares from mobile carts and even, in some cases, blasting music to announce their arrival. For many Thais, this is the taste of their childhood.

The 60-year-old ice cream parlor known as Nuttaporn is not a purveyor of the ice cream sandwich, but their hand-churned ice cream, made from coconut milk using old family recipes, has been beloved by Bangkokians practically since ice cream came to Thailand. Eschewing the mall chain outlets and fancy cafes of similarly famous eateries, this taciturn group of ladies still sells their wares out of an open-air shack in the Old Town outfitted with two or three tables in front. Some of the flavors, like mango and durian, are seasonal, but perpetual standbys include Thai tea, coffee, and of course, coconut milk.

If mango is not in season, I always order coconut milk, and am reminded by the owner's terse directive to choose the roasted peanut toppings to go with it; she claimed that nothing else enhanced the flavor properly. But if left to my own devices, I would happily order the Asian plum seeds, the coconut sticky rice, and even the corn, which Thais consider a dessert.

Ode to Local Neighborhood Drinks Vendors

Everyone who lives in Bangkok has a local drinks vendor, someone who sells iced coffee and/or tea, or even a few juices, on a street corner close to their home. Mine was named Yai Nang (Grandma Nang), and she recently passed away aged 84 years old, after working the area across the street from my house for 50 years.

Yai Nang had always been a drinks vendor, selling glasses of (highly) sweetened Thai coffee to passersby for decades. She fixed on her spot early, choosing it because it was right next to a *klong* (canal) that ran perpendicular to Sukhumvit Road, formerly considered the "boonies" or suburbs of Bangkok. The canal had a little bridge across it leading to the house that I live in now. All along the canal were similar houses, all belonging to members of the same family.

Yai Nang saw more than her share of changes while working her little patch of Bangkok, the same kind of changes that have turned the little "Venice of the East" into a sprawling megacity. The canal was paved over and made into a narrow road. Then one by one, the houses along the road were sold, many converted into apartment buildings. The big parcel of land at the end of the road was sold to a development company that turned it into a shopping complex. Today, the little road that was once a *klong* sees two-way traffic at all hours of the day, hosting sticky traffic jams on weekends when Thais are eager to get to the mall.

The shopping mall brought a lot of business to the area, cafes and restaurants. Demand for Yai Nang's particular blend of iced sweetened coffee waned, forcing her to sell odds and ends: eggs, instant noodles, bottles of water. Yet she persevered, a distinctive figure on a busy road, one of the last remaining relics of a time when Bangkok was a city of canals. In early 2022, she passed away from COVID.

Thai-style Iced Coffee

Yai Nang sold iced coffee in my neighborhood for 50 years. In her last months, I would often see her dozing by the side of the road. Whenever I see Thai iced coffee I think of her.

SERVES 2 ◦ **PREP TIME** ◦ **COOKING TIME: 20 MINUTES**

2 cups (500 ml) strong black coffee
Ice cubes
1 can sweetened condensed milk
   (add to taste)
Ground cardamom

Brew your coffee and wait until it reaches room temperature or chill it for about 10–15 minutes in the refrigerator before adding it to two cups full of ice.

Add the condensed milk to taste—the sweeter it is, the more "authentic" it is. Add a pinch of ground cardamom to each cup before serving.

Thai Iced Tea

This tea is creamy and sweet yet has the aroma and tang of tea leaves, thanks to the fermented Ceylon tea. It is typically red in color, but now Thai tea manufacturers have taken to dying the mix orange in keeping with what is seen as the characteristic color of Thai tea (like a very light caramel or the color of the wood in an upscale men's shoe store). Cha Tra Mue (cha-thai.com/en/) is probably the most famous brand of tea mix in Thailand but if you can't source it, substitutions are listed below courtesy of thespruceeats.com.

SERVES 2 ◦ **PREP TIME: 5-10 MINUTES** ◦ **COOKING TIME: 15 MINUTES**

Tea Mixture:

4 cups (1 l) water
6 heaping tablespoons Thai tea mix (like Cha Tra Mue). If you can't find Cha Tra Mue steep the following in 4 cups (1 l) water: 4 tablespoons loose-leaf black tea (or 4 tea bags), 2 star anise pod, 4 cardamom pods, 1 cinnamon stick, 4 cloves, pinch of turmeric, ½ vanilla bean or 1 teaspoon extract (almond extract may be substituted), tamarind powder, to taste (if you can get it)

Ice Tea Per Serving:

½ cup (100 ml) prepared Thai tea mix
3 tablespoons sweetened condensed milk
3 tablespoons milk or cream
Ice cubes

To make the tea: boil 4 cups of water. Once the water is boiling, put in the tea mix and keep boiling for 3-4 minutes. Take off the heat and place in a container to cool down.

Make the **Iced Tea** once the tea is cooled. Distribute the ice into individual glass. Combine ½ cup Thai tea mix with the condensed milk and milk or cream. Shake well and pour over the ice cubes.

Morning Ginger Drink

My husband has this every morning instead of coffee. He insists on it being homemade, and not from a powder bought from the supermarket. He says it gives him energy and keeps him from getting hungry up until noon. It's one of the very few high-maintenance things about him so I am happy to oblige him on making this, 5 liters at a time. Obviously, when we do make this, the whole kitchen smells of ginger, which is a good or bad thing, depending on your fondness for it. You need to use as mature a ginger root as you can find.

SERVES 4 • PREP TIME: 10 MINUTES • COOKING TIME: 2 HOURS

4 cups (1 liter) of water
Ginger, large hand sized root
   (8 oz/200 g) peeled, the older the
   better
Sugar or honey, to taste (optional)

Cut up the ginger and place in a big pot of water on the stove. Simmer over low heat for at least 2 hours, until the water is infused with the ginger.

Drain and drink hot immediately, or save in the freezer for whenever you need it. If you prefer it a little sweet, just add a teaspoon of sugar or honey.

This ginger drink, when sweetened, is also a good base for fresh tofu and deep-fried dough bits—a common street food breakfast.

Refreshing Lime Soda

My friend Gareth thought it was hilarious that I was writing a recipe for limeade (known in Thai as *manao soda*), to which I responded, hey, sometimes you need a recipe for stuff like this. You never know! In any case, I like my limeade with both salt and sugar—I think they amplify each other's flavors best—and I hope you will too.

SERVES 2 • PREP TIME: 5 MINUTES • COOKING TIME: 5 MINUTES

½ cup (125 ml) lime juice (fresh
   preferable)
1 cup (250 ml) soda water
1 teaspoon salt
Ice cubes

Syrup

1 cup (250 ml) water
1 cup (200 g) sugar

Make the **Syrup** by heating the water and sugar in a small pot and lightly boil for 3-5 minutes until a simple syrup forms. Set aside to cool.

Add the lime juice, soda water together with 1 cup (250 ml) Syrup. Add the salt. Taste for seasoning. It should be equal parts salty and sweet.

Pour over 2 highball glasses filled with ice cubes.

Thai-style Gin Fizz

This cocktail was created by my friend Dwight Turner of courageouskitchen.org. Dwight is a keen mixologist and this drink is as amiable as he is, going well with lemongrass, galangal, kaffir lime leaf or, best of all, roselle syrup.

SERVES 1 • PREP TIME: 5 MINUTES • COOKING TIME: 2 MINUTES

20 oz (60 ml) gin
2 tablespoons lime juice
1–2 bird's eye chilies, deseeded and sliced (or to taste)
1 teaspoon shaved palm sugar
Splash of bitters (optional)
Pinch of salt (optional)
1–3 aromatics or herbs, muddled or pounded (lemongrass, kaffir lime leaf, galangal and/or 1–2 tablespoons roselle syrup*)
Soda water, to taste
Ice cubes

Shake together all the ingredients and strain and pour into individual glass over some ice cubes. Garnish with whatever aromatic or herb you were using. Add soda water to taste. Enjoy.

*If roselle syrup is not available, you can make your own by boiling sugar and strong hibiscus/roselle tea together to make a simple syrup.

Thai Cooking Terms

In English alphabetical order, not Thai, corresponding to the romanizations used by the author)

Aharn General term for food

Budu Southern Thai equivalent of *kapi*, or shrimp paste, made of fermented fish parts

Chak To pull, as in to "pull" flavor out of ingredients

Dum Black, as in *puu dum*, or "black crab"

Foy Threads or something that looks like threads, such as *foy tong*

Gang A soup or curry, or the act of making a soup or curry out of something

Hoy Shellfish

Inter Thai slang for "international," as in *aharn inter*, or international food

Jiew Usually in reference to eggs, the act of making an omelet (ie to *jiew kai*). By reversing the order, you get *kai jiew*, the omelet.

Kiew To cook something slowly over a low flame

Kua To toast in a pan

Larb The act of making a minced salad. Again, it can be both a verb and a noun.

Mieng A type of dish involving small ingredients that can be put together and rolled into a leaf by the diner

Nao Literally, "rotten," but usually used in reference to something fermented (see: *tua nao*, or fermented soybean disc) (not to be confused with *nao*, or cold, which has a different tone in the Thai language)

Ob To bake

Pad To fry

Pla A type of spicy warm salad to which numerous julienned herbs are added such as kaffir lime leaves, lemongrass and cilantro leaves.

Ron Hot or heat

Rot Flavor

Sieb To pierce, like in forming a kebab or skewer

Thom To boil

Thum To pound in a mortar and pestle

Woon To form into a jelly, or when a noun, the jelly itself

Yang To grill

Index

Acknowledgments

Chawadee

This book started out as a way for Lauren Taylor and me to collaborate on something. So first and foremost, I'd like to thank Lauren. I still vividly remember our first drinks date by the Viaduct in Auckland. I'd also like to thank my husband and his family for humoring me. Thanks as well go to the culinary talents of Somporn Lalaeng and Praweephan Saiputong. My parents also get a shout-out, as do my long-suffering children, who were periodically neglected as this book came together. This book would also not have been possible without the people at Tuttle, Eric Oey, Doug Sanders and June Chong, and Galen Yeo, who helped with the proposal. And finally, all the other wonderful people who contributed to the recipes and essays in this book out of the kindness of their hearts: Chris Schultz, Tawn Chatchavalvong, Natayada na Songkhla, Chef McDang, Kesinee Bunchandranon, Dwight Turner, Panisha Chanwilai, Mark Wiens, Francisco Vaz Patto, Kevin Colleary, David Thompson, Joe Napol, Dylan Jones, Bo Songvisava, Jarrett Wrisley, Chef Black, Phil Cornwel-Smith, Tom Vityakul, Sujira Pongmon, Andy Ricker, Subphachittra Dinakara Sukarawan, Hanuman Aspler, Chin Chongtong, Donald Wilson, Gen Greer, and Chef Ice.

Lauren

A massive thank you to Chawadee for bringing me on this wonderful culinary journey with you. During a year of lockdowns and restricted travel, it was a joy to have Thailand come to life in my kitchen in Auckland. I am extremely grateful to my husband Noah Maffitt for all his culinary contributions to this book and for always being my rock. Thank you to my daughters, Cybella, Olivia and Lila for your cheerleading and willingness to eat all the recipes as they were tested. Special thanks to Kate Dobbin, Beatrice Carlson, Lisa Littleton, Daisy Lifton, Sari Hara for your help and support.

Finally, thank you Khen Tran for instilling in me my deep love for the making and sharing of good food.

"Books to Span the East and West"

Tuttle Publishing was founded in 1832 in the small New England town of Rutland, Vermont [USA]. Our core values remain as strong today as they were then—to publish best-in-class books which bring people together one page at a time. In 1948, we established a publishing outpost in Japan—and Tuttle is now a leader in publishing English-language books about the arts, languages and cultures of Asia. The world has become a much smaller place today and Asia's economic and cultural influence has grown. Yet the need for meaningful dialogue and information about this diverse region has never been greater. Over the past seven decades, Tuttle has published thousands of books on subjects ranging from martial arts and paper crafts to language learning and literature—and our talented authors, illustrators, designers and photographers have won many prestigious awards. We welcome you to explore the wealth of information available on Asia at **www.tuttlepublishing.com.**

Published by Tuttle Publishing, an imprint of Periplus Editions (HK) Ltd

www.tuttlepublishing.com

Copyright © 2023 Chawadee Nualkhair

ISBN 978-0-8048-5558-7

Distributed by
North America, Latin America & Europe
Tuttle Publishing
364 Innovation Drive, North Clarendon, VT 05759-9436 U.S.A.
Tel: 1 (802) 773-8930; Fax: 1 (802) 773-6993
info@tuttlepublishing.com; www.tuttlepublishing.com

Asia Pacific
Berkeley Books Pte. Ltd.
3 Kallang Sector #04-01, Singapore 349278
Tel: (65) 6741-2178; Fax: (65) 6741-2179
inquiries@periplus.com.sg; www.tuttlepublishing.com

26 25 24 23   10 9 8 7 6 5 4 3 2 1
Printed in China   2301EP

Photo Credits